ENGLISH Alive

Level 5

Barry Scholes and Gill Atha

Contents

Collins Educational

UNIT 1   Living Together

Read this passage carefully.

Suddenly there was a big row. He looked back over the wall in time to see Bobby Whitehead, and Patsy Broome, and the three little 'uns, all leap out from their hidey-hole and start bunging bricks. The air was full of them, and the little Pakistani kids just stood there for something like ages, and the rocks flying past their ears and bouncing off the soggy ground all round them. It was a miracle that none of them got hit, but they didn't seem to have the sense to do anything about it. Bernard the Black Hand almost forgot he was only there as a spy. He very nearly leapt up and yelled at them to run.

Bobby Whitehead and his lot were yelling all right, though. And they started to move slowly forward as they kept up the bombardment of stones. Some of the little kids started to dart about, as if they didn't know which way to turn. Bernard saw a rock bounce off the shoulder of a little girl of about five, and she fell into the cold mud, crying. Another little girl bent down to try and help her, with her long black pigtail hanging right down into a puddle. Two of the boys had started to pelt across towards the wire fence, and the hail of bricks followed them. It was a real rout.

Out of the corner of his eye again, Bernard saw a flashing movement at the same time as he heard a loud shout. He turned right, to see the Shofiq lad come roaring out of the garden of an old dumpy house like an express train. He'd dropped the wallbrick and picked up something that looked like a length of old rubber hose. It was about ten feet long, and grey, and an inch thick. What's more, he was swinging it round his head, round and round, faster and faster, as he ran.

Bernard was amazed. The lad was swaying with the weight of the hose whizzing round his head, sort of rocking as he ran. If it had gone much faster he would have taken off for sure, he looked so much like a helicopter. He shot towards Bobby Whitehead's lot at a terrific lick, yelling the top of his head off as he ran. The hail of rocks at the little kids stopped. They all got their wits back at once, even the girl that had been hit. They flashed across the croft bawling, a group of little frightened mice.

Bobby Whitehead shouted something, and Patsy Broome bent down to pick up a lump of iron at her feet. But it was too late, much too late. Bernard watched fascinated as the Pakistani lad got closer. The little 'uns dropped their bricks and ran. Pat looked at Bobby and she'd gone white. He just stared, shocked, as the helicopter whirled towards him. He opened his mouth. Patsy pulled back her arm as if she was going to bung the lump of iron, then she dropped it. She started to back away. She looked terrified. The whooshing noise of the whirling hosepipe came clearly to Bernard's ears. The Pakistani lad's mouth was open, his face all twisted up. Big Patsy turned on her heels and ran.

It was obvious to Bernard that Bobby Whitehead was going to scarper too, it just had to happen. But he didn't get the chance. His gob was still wide open and he looked as if he'd wet himself. As he half turned, looking to where Pat was whistling over the croft towards the school, the helicopter arrived. As Bobby got his legs into action the hose-pipe-end came whirling round, whooshing as it came. The tail-end of it caught him right across the side of the head, and he went down into a puddle with an icy splash.

Bernard, his own mouth wide open in admiration and horror, looked at the still form of the terrible Bobby Whitehead. His face was like a sheet and he wasn't moving. From under the hair above his ear a long curtain of blood started to flow.

The Pakistani lad had let go of the hosepipe and rubbed his hands on his jeans. He walked over to Bobby Whitehead's body and looked down at it. Then he looked towards the school and started to walk towards it. He was still panting, but that was all. Bernard skirted the fallen giant and scuttled in by a different gate. He felt quite peculiar; not at all like a secret agent.
(From *My Mate Shofiq* by Jan Needle)

Answer these questions in as much detail as possible.
1   Why do you think Bobby Whitehead and his friends were throwing stones at the other children?
2   Why do you think Bernard was there?
3   How did he feel about what was happening?
4   Why do you think Bobby left it too late to escape?
5   How do you feel about Shofiq's attack on Bobby? Give reasons for your answers.
6   What do you think will happen next in the story? Give reasons for your answer.

Writing
Retell the events of the story in your own words.
Try to include as much detail as possible.

Characters

Shofiq Rahman   Bobby Whitehead   Patsy Broome   Bernard Kershaw

Think about what you know of these characters from the passage. What words would you use to describe them?

Write the names of the four characters as headings in your book. Under each heading write words to describe each character. Here are some to start you off.

aggressive	gentle	spiteful	cruel	bullying
cowardly	helpful	brave	mean	kind
terrified	frightened			

Friendship

To think and talk about

1   Do you have a best friend? Who is it? What is it about that person that makes him/her your best friend?
2   How do you decide who your friends are?

To write about

Make a list of your friends' names. Next to each name give reasons why you like them.
   This is what Elliot wrote about his friends.

Jason Peters   My best friend. I've known him since we first came to school. We enjoy the same things, and support the same football team.

Carl Donohue   He doesn't go to our school, but we go to the same judo class. He's very strong and we have a good laugh together.

Glynn Erran   Glynn is my pen friend. We met on holiday in Wales. He is one year older than I am. We share the same interests.

Chi-Lee Lung   He is the best footballer in school, and he's brilliant at drawing. I sit next to him in class.

Definitions

In the dictionary a friend is defined as "someone you know well and like a lot" or "a person on the same side in a struggle".
How would you define a friend? Write down your definition.
How would you define "friendship" and "friendliness"?

A Friendship Poem

You could use the definitions suggested by your group to make a list poem, like this:

Friendship

Friendship is the best thing anyone can have.
With a friend you can never be lonely.
A friend is someone special, someone who is always with you,
Someone you can trust.
A friend is someone who shares your secrets,
And always knows just what you're thinking.
A friend is someone who doesn't mind when you're in a bad mood,
But cheers you up with a smile and a joke,
Making you feel good.
A friend should be like my dog, Sparky.

Word Study
Prefix and Suffix
Many long words are in fact made up of more common short words (root words) with a beginning (*prefix*) or ending (*suffix*) added to them.

A Prefixes
The most common prefixes are **un-, in-, mis-** and **dis-**. They are used to give the root word an opposite meaning.

root word		prefix + root word	=	new word	
honest		dis + honest		dishonest	

Add a prefix to give each of these root words its opposite meaning.
Use a dictionary if you are uncertain about any of them.

1	appear	5	sufficient	9	fit	13	believe
2	colour	6	correct	10	understand	14	acceptable
3	obey	7	eaten	11	perfect	15	sure
4	possible	8	visible	12	forgettable		

B Suffixes
A suffix is added to the end of a root word to change its meaning.

1 Write out the root words and suffixes for these words. The first one has been done for you.

                                root word   *suffix*
   a) friendship = friend + ship
   b) likeable   =
   c) foreigner
   d) lifeless
   e) bravery
   f) ghost-like
   g) watery
   h) uppermost

2 Copy and complete these sentences by adding a suffix to the underlined root word.

   a) The Hit Boys tried to <u>appear</u> calm and confident when they made their first _____ on Top of the Pops.
   b) The broken cup was _____. Jamie had to <u>use</u> another one.
   c) They were unable to <u>drink</u> the water. It was not _____.
   d) Lucy's doctor told her to <u>rest</u>, but she spent a very _____ night.
   e) The _____ hoisted the <u>sail</u> and set out to sea.

Falling Out
To think and talk about
Children often fall out with each other. Why do they do this? Have you ever fallen out with a friend? What did you do? Why did it happen? How did you feel? Did you make friends again? How did you do it?

To write about
Imagine how you would feel if all your friends fell out with you. Write a story saying what happened to make you fall out and how you all made friends again.

A Friend in Need

Here is a further extract from *My Mate Shofiq*. You might like to re-read the extract which opened this unit before you continue with the story.

When everyone was quiet, Miss Todd put on her encouraging smile for the lad. He didn't smile back, although he was looking at her full in the face. After a while she went pinkish.

'Well, Shofiq,' she said. 'And what was all that about, do you think?'

He opened up his hands in a funny, foreign way.

'I don't know, Miss,' he said.

There was a murmur from the class, instantly hushed.

'Oh come now Shofiq,' Miss Todd went on. 'That won't do, now will it! Patricia Broome comes in looking for somebody quite definite, and says you attacked Robert Whitehead with a lead pipe, and you know nothing about it! Does that sound entirely likely?'

'I don't know, Miss,' said the lad quietly. 'But I'll have to tell the headmaster something, so I'll leave it till then, eh?'

Miss Todd went pinker yet. The Pakistani boy had a funny way of talking to grown-ups; Bernard would never have dared to go anywhere near it. He had a right strong accent, too — not Pakistani, but Lancashire, just like the rest of them, just like Bernard himself. Miss Todd was getting angry, losing her rag, anyone could tell that.

'That is a very silly attitude to take, Shofiq Rahman,' she snapped. 'It is apparent to me that you have been fighting, and fighting with weapons. That is not a nice thing, nor is it Br . . . allowed. You are going to get into very serious trouble if you go on like this, and I wish to know all about it. Now! Tell me exactly what happened!'

The whole class was entranced. It was absolutely smashing, to see Miss lose her rag over the way he was cheeking her. Then the Pakistani lad gave a kind of shrug with his shoulders.

'I'd rather say nowt, Miss, if you don't mind,' he said, almost in a whisper. 'I'm quite willing to take what's coming from Mr Ellis.'

An odd feeling was coming over Bernard. He hadn't the faintest idea what this daft lad thought he was doing, but he knew it meant trouble. Miss Todd was a right bad-tempered old crow, and there was no doubt she was going to go up the wall in a minute or two, go really sky-high off her undercarriage. She thought he'd been doing a bit of private battering, and now he was being smart about it. Bernard didn't know why he just didn't speak out, say what Bobby Whitehead had been up to, but he wasn't going to, obviously. Kids all over the room were nudging each other in glee, making sure she didn't see them at it, because she'd turn on them then, no danger. It was a right pantomime, to see the Pakistani get himself in lumber.

'I will give you one more chance to be polite and sensible, Shofiq Rahman,' said Miss Todd icily. 'And then I wash my hands of the matter. Have you been indulging in violent fighting, or is there something else behind all this?'

Bernard could see that the eyes of the standing boy were very bright. To his amazement he felt tears prick his own eyes. He bit his lip. He was confused, dry-mouthed. He suddenly shot his

Sequencing Sentences

These sentences are about both parts of the story, but they have been arranged in the wrong order. Copy them out in their correct sequence.

> Bernard watched, but wanted to tell the Pakistanis to run.
> The Pakistani boy hit Bobby with the hosepipe.
> Bobby began throwing bricks at the Pakistani children.
> Patsy Broome was sent to fetch Shofiq. A rock hit a young girl and she fell down.
> Shofiq would not tell the teacher about the fight.
> Shofiq ran out of a nearby garden.
> Miss Todd asked the boys to explain to Mr. Ellis.
> Patsy ran away.
> Bernard told Miss Todd all about the fight.

hand up. Well, he didn't. It shot up of its own accord, there wasn't any way he could stop it.

'Please, Miss,' he said. 'It weren't him, Miss. It weren't his fault. It were the Whitehead lot. They were Paki . . . They were bunging . . . They were . . .'

The tension was electric. The Pakistani lad sat down, plonk, without being told. There was a low murmur of voices, which faded away as Miss Todd waved her hand in the air.

'Oh?' she said, in a completely different tone of voice. 'What's this, Bernard? Robert Whitehead was what?'

In for a penny, in for a pound. Bernard gulped unhappily.

'He were Paki-bashing, Miss. Him and Pa . . . Him and some others. They were bunging bricks. That Sho . . . that lad there waded in to 'em and stopped 'em.'

Miss Todd was smiling.

'Well well,' she said. 'I never thought I'd live to see the day. Well well.'

Bernard sat there, bright red, feeling a proper duck-egg. The eyes of the other kids bored into him, in a shocked, almost horrified, way. Bernard Kershaw sticking up for a Paki? Never!

Miss Todd rapped abruptly on her desk lid.

'Right,' she said. 'Off you go then. Cut along with your friend now and speak to Mr Ellis quite firmly and clearly about what you saw. I have a feeling he will be exceedingly interested to hear it.'

Your friend! There was a titter from the kids around him. Bernard's face began to burn. The Pakistani boy was waiting by the door, not looking at anything, just standing, waiting. Miss Todd jerked her head sideways.

'Come! Get along with you now.'

Bernard went. When he reached the Pakistani lad they left the room together, walked along the disinfectanty corridors in silence. Oh my God, he thought: why didn't I keep my rotten mouth shut!

(From *My Mate Shofiq* by Jan Needle)

1 Were you surprised at Bernard's actions? Give reasons for your answer.
2 Why do you think Shofiq was unwilling to explain himself?
3 What do you think Miss Todd was originally going to say when she began: "That is not a nice thing, nor is it Br . . . allowed"?
   Why do you think she changed her mind?
4 What did she think Shofiq had been up to?
5 Why do you think the other children were shocked when Bernard stuck up for Shofiq?
6 What does that tell you about Bernard's attitude before these events occurred?

Changing Attitudes
To think and talk about
1 Look back at the description you made of the four main characters after the first part of the story. Has reading the second part made you change your mind about any of them? Can you say why?
2 Examine your own attitudes and those of the group to these controversial areas:
   a) racial equality b) sex equality.
      Write down the main points of your group's discussion so that you may use these ideas in a debate.

Venn Diagrams

Look at the diagram showing the friends of Sujata and Carole. It is called a Venn diagram after the person who invented it. It shows lots of information in a very simple way.

A Venn Diagram of Sujata and Carole's friends

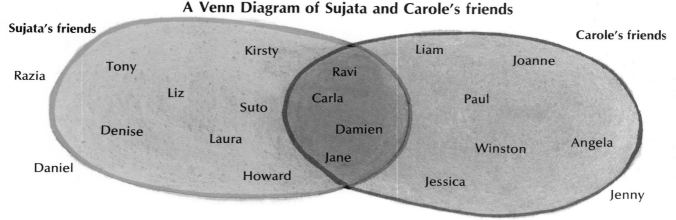

All the names in the *red* circle are the friends of Sujata.
All the names in the *blue* circle are friends of Carole.
The names that appear in the *purple* sector, where the two circles overlap, are friends of both girls.
The names that are outside the circles are friends of neither girl.
NOTE: Each child's name appears only once.

Study the diagram and use it to answer these questions.
1 How many friends has Carole?
2 How many more friends has Sujata?
3 How many friends do the two girls share?
4 Whose friend is **a)** Carla? **b)** Joanne? **c)** Razia?
5 Is Sujata friends with **a)** Suto? **b)** Winston? **c)** Damien?
6 Draw a similar Venn diagram showing your own and your partner's friends. Don't forget to include names of some people who are not your friends.
7 Here is a Venn diagram showing the hobbies of three children. Study it carefully and then make up your own questions for a friend to answer.

A Venn Diagram of Hobbies

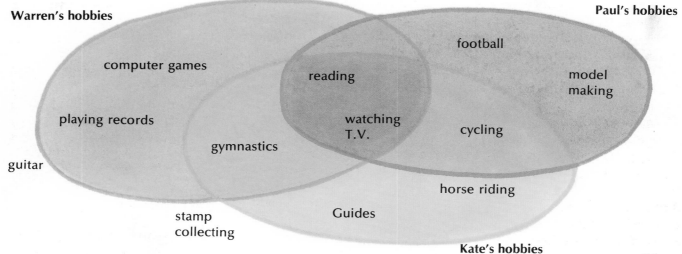

Say It Another Way

Read these sentences carefully. Put a word in the gap to make the second sentence mean the same as the first one.

1 Judith is friendly towards Samantha. Judith and Samantha are good _____.
2 I live at 49, Chichester Close. 49, Chichester Close is my _____.
3 Jonathan, Theo and Ben all have similar interests. They are all _____ in the same things.
4 The balloon stayed up in the air. It did not come _____.
5 Joanne's mum did well in her driving test. She _____ her driving test.
6 Everybody in our class likes Hywell Jones. He is very _____.
7 Shofiq hit the boy on purpose. He hit him _____.
8 Gail was at a loose end. She had _____ to do.
9 Mr. Carraway is hard up. He is _____ of money.
10 The two neighbours were very argumentative. They always had lots of _____. They _____ all the time.

Writing
Write an amusing story about two neighbours who argued continually. Say why they argued and if they ever stopped. Think of a good title for your story.

Idioms
Idioms are expressions whose meaning it is difficult to guess from the words used.
For example: The Lady had money to burn.

This doesn't mean what it appears to say, but only that she has a great deal of money and spends it freely.

1 Match each idiom with its meaning. The first one has been done for you.

Idiom	Meaning
The lady had money to burn.	The boy was in serious trouble.
I am up to my eyes with homework.	You have just said what I was going to say.
It was raining cats and dogs.	She always keeps her promises.
Money burns holes in his pockets.	I have lots of homework to do.
You have just taken the words right out of my mouth.	He was very awkward and clumsy.
Her word is her bond.	She has a great deal of money and spends it freely.
He was like a bear with a sore head.	It was raining heavily.
The boy was in hot water.	They decided to end their quarrelling.
Denny had two left feet.	He was in a very bad mood.
The neighbours decided to bury the hatchet.	He spends his money very quickly.

Write your own sentences to mean the same as these.
1 Brother and sister were tarred with the same brush.
2 Two heads are better than one.
3 The teacher can't make head or tail of his work.

Bullying

I've Got an Apple Ready

My hair's tightly plaited;
I've a bright blue bow;
I don't want my breakfast,
And now I must go.

My satchel's on my shoulder;
Nothing's out of place;
And I've got an apple ready,
Just in case.

So it's 'Good-bye, Mother!'
And off down the street;
Briskly at first
On pit-a-pat feet,

But slow and more slow
As I reach that tarred
Trackway that runs
By Hodson's Yard;

For it's there sometimes
Bill Craddock waits for me
To snatch off my beret
And throw it in a tree.

Bill Craddock leaning
On Hodson's rails;
Bill with thin hands
And dirty nails;

Bill with a front tooth
Broken and bad;
His dark eyes cruel,
And somehow sad.

Often there are workmen,
And then he doesn't dare;
But this morning I feel
He'll be there.

At the corner he will pounce . . .
But quickly I'll say
'Hallo, Bill! have an apple!' —
In an ordinary way.

I'll push it in his hand
And walk right on;
And when I'm round the corner
I'll run!
(John Walsh)

About the poem
1 Did you like the poem? Say why.
2 Describe in detail what the girl in the poem is like.
3 Do you think the girl's parents know about Bill Craddock? What makes you think so?
4 How do you think Bill Craddock feels while he is waiting for the girl?
5 Why do you think Bill Craddock behaves like this? Give reasons for your answer.

Bullying
To think and talk about
1 Have you ever bullied or been bullied by someone? What happened? How did you feel about it?
2 Would you choose someone like Bill Craddock to be your friend? Say why.
3 Why did the girl give Bill an apple? What would you have done if you had been the girl in the poem?
4 How can you stop people from bullying you?

To write about
Write a story called "I'm going to get you, Bill Craddock" in which you plot your revenge on the bully. Explain your plan and say how Bill reacts. Is your plan successful?

Looking at Both Sides

When people argue or disagree about something you may need to help them sort it out. You can't do this until you have heard both sides of the story. Even then it may be difficult to find out who was to blame.

Look at what these children have been arguing about. Decide for yourself who, if anyone, is in the wrong and say how you would sort it out.

To think about

1 Is it only children who fall out and argue?
2 What do adults argue about? Is it bars of chocolate and broken watches?

The Bully Asleep

The Bully Asleep

This afternoon, when grassy
Scents through the classroom crept,
Bill Craddock laid his head
Down on his desk, and slept.

The children came round him:
Jimmy, Roger, and Jane;
They lifted his head timidly
And let it sink again.

"Look, he's gone sound asleep,
  Miss,"
Said Jimmy Adair;
"He stays up all the night, you see;
His mother doesn't care."

"Stand away from him children.".
Miss Andrews stooped to see.
"Yes, he's asleep; go on
With your writing, and let him be."

"Now's a good chance!"
  whispered Jimmy;
And he snatched Bill's pen and hid it.
"Kick him under the desk, hard;
He won't know who did it."

"Fill all his pockets with rubbish —
Paper, apple-cores, chalk."
So they plotted, while Jane
Sat wide-eyed at their talk.

Not caring, not hearing,
Bill Craddock he slept on;
Lips parted, eyes closed —
Their cruelty gone.

"Stick him with pins!"
  muttered Roger.
"Ink down his neck!" said Jim.
But Jane, tearful and foolish,
Wanted to comfort him.
(John Walsh)

About the poem

1   In what ways is this poem similar to "I've Got an Apple Ready"?
2   In what ways is it different?
3   What do the boys in the poem want to do to Bill? Why?
4   What do you notice about the behaviour of the boys in this poem and that of Bill Craddock in the previous one?
5   Why do you think the poet describes Jane as foolish? Do you agree with him? Give a reason for your answer.
6   Who do you think has the right idea of what to do: the boys, the teacher or Jane?
7   What would you have done to Bill?
8   Why does the poet mention the fact that Bill's mother doesn't care? Does this change your earlier opinion of him? Say why.

To think and talk about

1   Does this poem give you a better understanding of why Bill behaves the way he does? Do you think his behaviour has anything to do with his home life? Is it possible that there are reasons for the bad behaviour of people you know?
2   Think about something bad you may once have done. Why did you do it? Was it for attention? To get something you wanted? Or was it for some other reason?

Poems Into Plays

Look at these excerpts from drama scripts that three children have written.

Mum: Sit still, Jane, while I put this bow in your hair.
Jane: But, Mum....
Mum: And look - you haven't even finished your breakfast!
Jane: I don't want it, Mum. I'm not hungry.
Mum: Are you all right?
Jane: Of course. Look, I must go. Oh, I'll take an apple with me. In case I get hungry later. Bye, Mum.

Bill: Right then, squirt. I've been waiting for you. Come on, give us that soppy hat.
Jane: Hello, Bill! Have an apple!
Bill: Cor! Hey, come back! I haven't finished with you yet.

Roger: Hey, look. Bully Bill's asleep!
Miss A: What's the matter? What's going on?
Jimmy: Look. He's gone sound asleep, Miss.
Miss A: Dear me!
Jimmy: He stays up all night. His mother doesn't care.

These short scenes have been adapted from the two John Walsh poems about Bill Craddock. Look how the children have featured the characters from the poems and used their actual spoken words, together with lines they have invented for the play version.

Read the extracts aloud with members of your group. Do the lines sound like real speech? Can you think of any ways to improve them?

Write your own play about either or both of these poems. Think what words the characters would really say. Read the line aloud to see if it sounds real. Think of a good title for your play.

13

Opinions

Although there are billions of people in the world, there are no two people exactly alike. Even identical twins do not necessarily think and feel the same. We all have different views and opinions about the things around us, yet we still manage to get on together. In fact the world would be a very dull place if we all shared the same opinions!

It is important to respect other people's opinions and viewpoints. They are just as valid as ours — even if we do not agree with them.

People such as politicians, advertisers and entertainers take opinions very seriously. They commission opinion polls to find what people are thinking.

Here is an opinion poll about popular entertainment.

OPINION POLL

Who's the Greatest?

Just enter the names of your favourite entertainers and return the coupon to us.

TV
Best children's TV programme ....
Best Comedy ....
Best Documentary ....
Best Drama Series ....
Best TV Personality ....
Best Actor ....
Best Actress ....

Music
Best Singer ....
Best Group ....
Best Single ....
Best Album ....

The public are invited to fill in the questionnaire and then send it in. The answers to the questions are recorded and used to find the most popular entertainer, singer, etc.

Here are the results of the opinion poll. Study them very carefully, together with the questionnaire, before answering the following questions.

Here are the results of our **Who's the Greatest?** opinion poll. The poll shows the two most popular choices in each category, together with the number of votes scored.

TV

Best children's TV programme: Janie! (2,247), Fat Cat (1,597)
Best Comedy: The Trudy McGraw Show (4,147), Every Good Turn (4,004)
Best Documentary: Local, National, International (3,103), Insight (2,776)
Best Drama Series: The Slaughterers (3,967), Breakthrough (3,877)
Best TV Personality: Les Knight (3,014), Basil Hall (2,100)
Best Actor: Douglas R. Stein (2,140), J. J. Johnstone (2,100)
Best Actress: Stella McCoy (4,160), Bambi Laferne (1,196)

Music

Best Singer: Chumley (Crocodile Mousse) (4,610), Carole Deakin (3,143)
Best Group: Crocodile Mousse (5,676), Ace is High (4,996)
Best Single: Gizzit 'ere (Crocodile Mousse) (6,016)
Sweet Dreams Turn Sour (The Lonely Hearts) (4,179)
Best Album: Make it Snappy! (Crocodile Mousse) (5,145)
60 Golden Glories (The Boomerangs) (4,171)

1 In which category was the programme "Janie!" voted the most popular?
2 What is the title of Crocodile Mousse's popular hit single?
3 How many votes did Les Knight achieve in the category of Best T.V. personality?
4 By how many votes did he beat Basil Hall?
5 Use the voting figures to work out what is the most popular television programme of all. Why do you think this is?
6 Can you think of any other categories that might have been added to the original opinion poll?
7 Ask a younger or older class to give their nominations. Check the results. Are they different from the opinions of your group. Why do you think this is so? What does this tell you about the results of opinion polls?

Changes of Opinion

To think and talk about

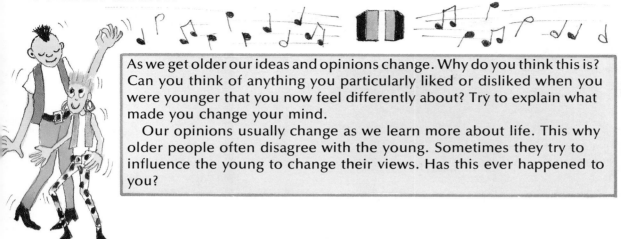

As we get older our ideas and opinions change. Why do you think this is? Can you think of anything you particularly liked or disliked when you were younger that you now feel differently about? Try to explain what made you change your mind.

Our opinions usually change as we learn more about life. This why older people often disagree with the young. Sometimes they try to influence the young to change their views. Has this ever happened to you?

Differences of Opinion
Read the views of these art critics.

WONDERFUL!

Mr. Aston
The "Mona Lisa" is without doubt the star of the gallery exhibition. It is one of the finest paintings ever done: the work of the most talented artist the world has ever known. It looks as good now as the day it was finished. No real art lover will want to miss this treat. It is a shame some of the other works of so-called art have been displayed so close to it. Their brash colours and ugly lines are an irritating distraction to the magnificent "Mona Lisa" centrepiece.

Mr. Dupont
I really cannot see what all the fuss is about. Lots of paintings in the exhibition outshine and outclass the dull and lifeless "Mona Lisa". The lively vibrant colours and shapes of some of the modern works are such a welcome change from the boring plain colours of "Mona". The modern work would have been a much more fitting centrepiece. In my opinion the "Mona Lisa" is as dead as its artist!

1 Which art critic prefers the modern work? What reasons does he give for his preference?
2 Read Mr. Aston's report again carefully. How much of it is fact and how much opinion?
3 Whose opinion, if any, do you agree with? Say why.

To think and talk about
How does each critic attempt to influence our opinions of the paintings?

15

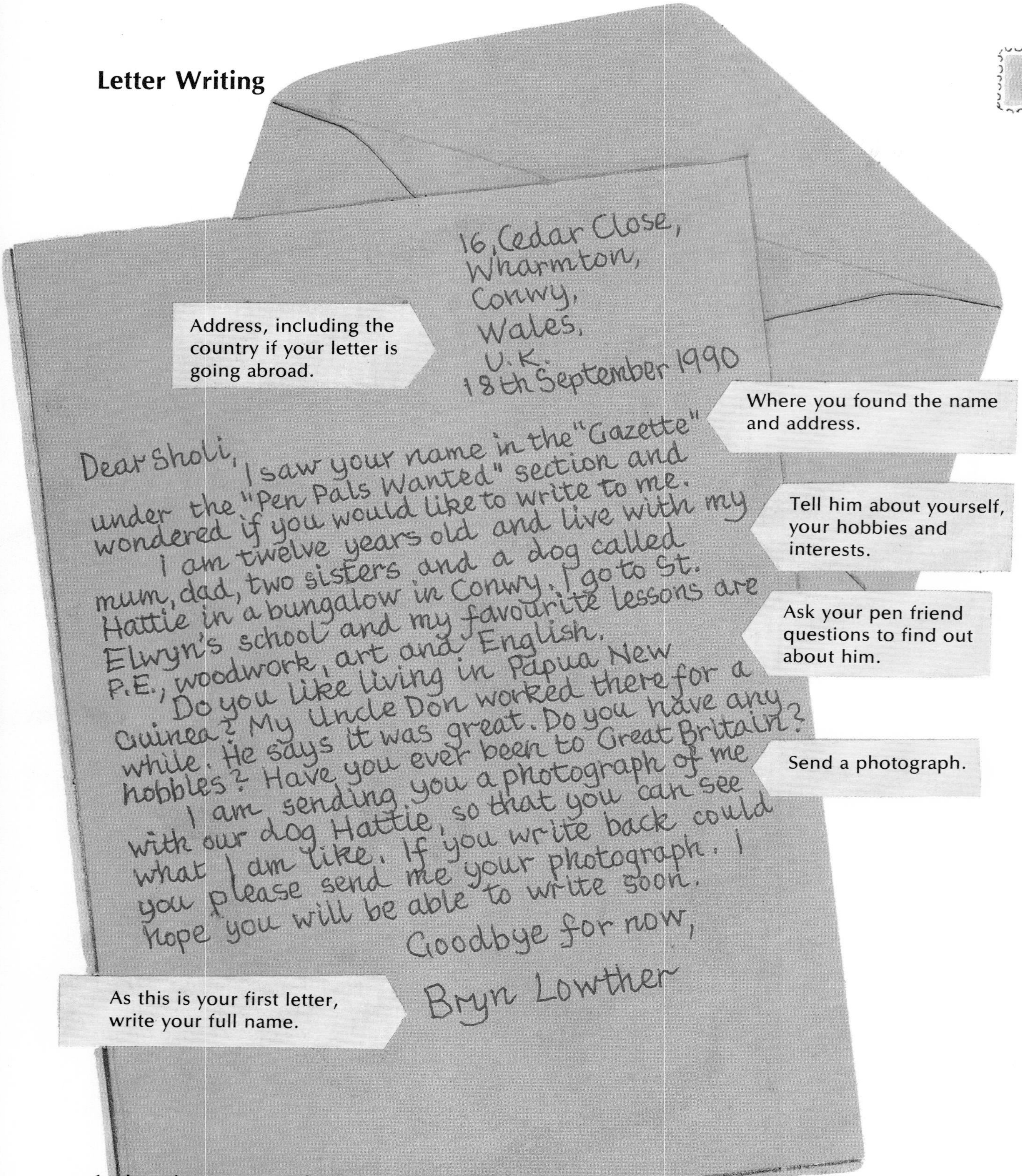

16, Cedar Close,
Wharmton,
Conwy,
Wales,
U.K.
18th September 1990

> Address, including the country if your letter is going abroad.

> Where you found the name and address.

Dear Sholi,
I saw your name in the "Gazette" under the "Pen Pals Wanted" section and wondered if you would like to write to me.
I am twelve years old and live with my mum, dad, two sisters and a dog called Hattie in a bungalow in Conwy. I go to St. Elwyn's school and my favourite lessons are P.E., woodwork, art and English.
Do you like living in Papua New Guinea? My Uncle Don worked there for a while. He says it was great. Do you have any hobbies? Have you ever been to Great Britain?
I am sending you a photograph of me with our dog Hattie, so that you can see what I am like. If you write back could you please send me your photograph. I hope you will be able to write soon.
Goodbye for now,

Bryn Lowther

> Tell him about yourself, your hobbies and interests.

> Ask your pen friend questions to find out about him.

> Send a photograph.

> As this is your first letter, write your full name.

1 Imagine you are Sholi. Write a reply to Bryn's letter answering his questions. Think of questions you would like to ask him.
2 Have you a pen friend? Addresses are sometimes printed in newspapers and magazines. Perhaps your teacher could help you find an address?
3 Record a sound letter on cassette. In what ways could this be made more exciting than a written letter? (Consider "sound pictures" of your hobbies, your school and your friends.)

We often write letters expressing opinions. This letter gives one person's opinion of animals in zoos. Look at how it is set out. What similarities and differences are there between this and Bryn's letter?

58 Ambleside Walk
Rolterton
Devon
RT7 1FV

28th July, 1990

Dear Madam,

I am writing to complain about the article in Saturday's "Chronicle" in which you say that more zoos should be opened.

I think the suggestion is cruel. Many of the animals are used to wandering free through jungles or across plains. They certainly cannot be happy in small concrete enclosures where they are cramped and often on their own. A good many of them are used to much warmer weather and must be miserable in our climate. I think your article was very selfish. We should put the animals' feelings first.

Yours faithfully,

Janette Barker

Janette Barker

To think and talk about

1 What do you think the newspaper said about zoos?
2 What do *you* think about zoos? What could you say in defence of them?

To write about

1 Decide which side of the argument you agree with and write a letter to the newspaper's editor telling her what you think.
2 Pretend you are the newspaper's editor and write a personal reply to Janette.

Envelopes

Don't forget to address your envelopes properly.
Use this envelope as a model to address an envelope to: **a)** your best friend; **b)** your head teacher; **c)** your parent.

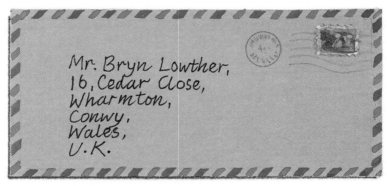

Mr. Bryn Lowther,
16, Cedar Close,
Wharmton,
Conwy,
Wales,
U.K.

Video Recordings

Making a video cassette recording can be a useful way of expressing points of view.

Plan and record a short sequence in which an interviewer asks your group their views on an issue such as keeping animals in zoos.

Each member of the group should consider his/her views in advance of the recording, but it is not necessary to rehearse lines. What should be planned and rehearsed are the order in which people are questioned and how the camera should record them.

Afterwards play back the recording and decide if the range of opinion within the group was fairly presented. If not, discuss improvements in interviewing and presentation techniques.

Make a second recording, without wiping the first one. Compare the two critically. What have you learned?

UNIT 2   Journeys

Journey to the End of the Earth

This is the true story of a famous journey to the South Pole. It was an expedition with a tragic end.

The continent of Antarctica had been charted by Captain James Cook in the 1770s, but more detailed knowledge of this icy wasteland was gained by Sir James Clark Ross in 1839 when he smashed his way through pack ice to a then unknown "shallow" sea which now bears his name. In January 1895 a Norwegian whaling captain named Kristensen put a boat and a few men ashore on Cape Adare in the Ross Sea. These first footsteps in the barren iceland caused great international interest and people yearned to explore the interior of this snowy desert to its very heart: the South Pole.

Robert Falcon Scott was one such person and in June 1910 he set out to achieve this goal, but he was not alone in the attempt. A Norwegian explorer named Roald Amundsen was also determined to be the first to reach the Pole. The race was on.

Scott reached Antarctica in October 1911, and on November 1st he set out across the Ross Ice Shelf. He used Siberian pit ponies to pull his sleds, but in the severe weather conditions many of the ponies sank in the snow and either died of cold or had to be shot to put an end to their misery.

On 4th January 1912 Scott and four companions set out to attempt the final stage of the journey, manhandling the sleds themselves. Conditions were harsh as the five men made their way over the ice and snow. Captain Scott kept a detailed diary of the attempt. Here is his entry for Tuesday, January 16th 1912.

Scott

Camp 68   Height: 9760 feet   **Temperature:** −23.3°

We started off in high spirits feeling that tomorrow would see us at our destination. About the second hour of that march Bowers' sharp eyes detected what he thought was a cairn*; he was uneasy about it but argued that it might be a sastragus**. Half an hour later he detected a black speck. We marched on and found it was a black flag tied to a sledge runner; nearer, the remains of a camp; sledge tracks and ski tracks and the clear traces of dogs' paws. This told us the whole story. Amundsen and his Norwegians have forestalled us and are the first at the Pole. It is a terrible disappointment and I am very sorry for my loyal companions. Tomorrow we must march on to the Pole and then hasten home with all the speed we can compass. All the daydreams must go; it will be a wearisome return.

Amundsen had arrived at the South Pole on December 14th 1911; over a month before Scott and his party! Imagine how disappointed and despondent the five men must have felt as they began to trudge their way back home. Worse, however, was to come; blizzards, accidents, frostbite, general weakness and scarce supplies all left their marks on the dispirited team.

On February 17th Petty Officer Evans died as a result of a fall into a crevasse and, exactly one month later, on his own birthday, Captain Oates, who was almost crippled with frostbite, took himself off into the polar night and certain death so that he would no longer be a burden to his friends.

Scott, Bowers and Wilson struggled on towards their much-needed supply depot. Fierce blizzards, however, trapped them inside their tent. Here, with hardly any food and not enough fuel to keep warm, Scott made his last entries in his diary.

The real thing that has stopped us is the awful weather and the unexpected cold towards the end of the journey . . . but for my own sake I do not regret this journey . . . Had we lived I would have had a tale to tell of the hardihood, endurance and courage of my friends . . . These rough notes and our dead bodies must tell the tale . . . it seems a pity but I do not think I can write more.

Their bodies were found eight months later — only sixteen miles away from the food depot that contained the supplies they needed for survival.

A cairn* with a cross made from two skis was built above their bodies and a huge cross bearing the five men's names was erected near the Ross Ice Barrier. It says: *To strive, To seek, To find, And Not to Yield.*

* *cairn:* a small pile of stones used as a landmark.
** *sastrugus:* a snow wave formed by the icy wind.

About the Passage

1 By how many days had Amundsen beaten Scott to the Pole?
2 What transport did Amundsen use on his journey to the Pole? Write the sentence that tells you this.
3 Imagine you are Bowers. Re-tell in your own words the events that led to the finding of the Norwegian camp.
4 Re-read Scott's last diary entries again. Imagine help was just outside as Scott wrote, and that he and his two friends were rescued. Write a diary entry saying what happened and how Scott felt.

Time Line

Use the information in the passage to help you complete this time line with the appropriate dates and events.

Journey to the End of the Earth: Timeline

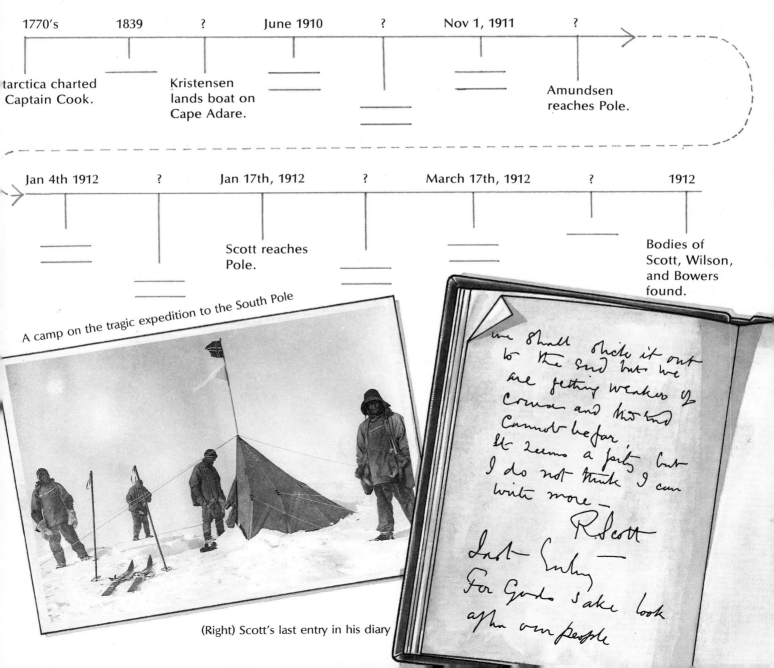

1770's   1839   ?   June 1910   ?   Nov 1, 1911   ?

tarctica charted   Kristensen   Amundsen
Captain Cook.   lands boat on   reaches Pole.
    Cape Adare.

Jan 4th 1912   ?   Jan 17th, 1912   ?   March 17th, 1912   ?   1912

    Scott reaches   Bodies of
    Pole.   Scott, Wilson,
        and Bowers
        found.

A camp on the tragic expedition to the South Pole

(Right) Scott's last entry in his diary

A Map of Antarctica

This is a map of Antarctica showing the routes taken by Scott and Amundsen on their journeys to the South Pole. Study the map carefully and use it to help you complete the activities below.

Things to do

1 Using the information on the map describe in detail the route to the Pole that was taken by Captain Scott.

2 We know that the Ross Ice Barrier, or Sea, was named after Sir James Clark Ross who was the first to enter this vast area of pack ice. From your knowledge of Scott's journey can you guess how these places got their names?

| Mt. Evans | Oates Land | King Edward VII Plateau |

3 Use your library, encyclopedias and reference books to find how these areas got their names:

| Beardmore Glacier | One Ton Depot | Adelie Land |
| King Haakon VII Plateau | Weddell Sea | Victoria Land |

4 Other names have been associated with Antarctic exploration. Use your reference material to find more about these intrepid explorers:

| Ernest Shackleton | Dr. Vivian Fuchs | Sir Edmund Hillary |

A Map of Amberhurst Village

Read very carefully this passage from *The Diddakoi* by Rumer Godden.

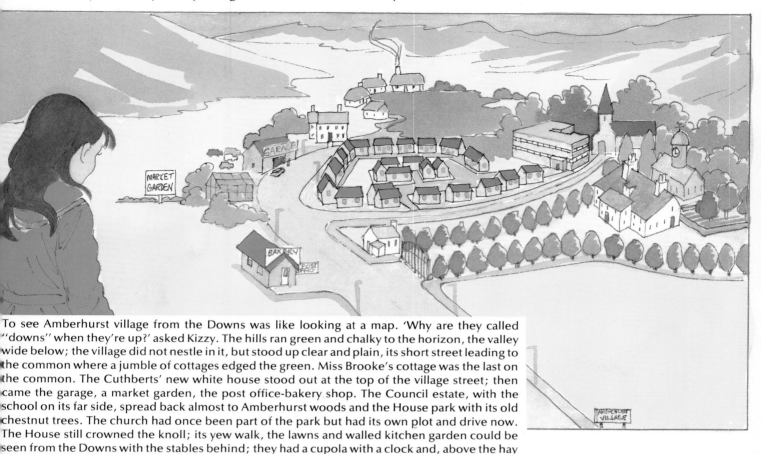

To see Amberhurst village from the Downs was like looking at a map. 'Why are they called "downs" when they're up?' asked Kizzy. The hills ran green and chalky to the horizon, the valley wide below; the village did not nestle in it, but stood up clear and plain, its short street leading to the common where a jumble of cottages edged the green. Miss Brooke's cottage was the last on the common. The Cuthberts' new white house stood out at the top of the village street; then came the garage, a market garden, the post office-bakery shop. The Council estate, with the school on its far side, spread back almost to Amberhurst woods and the House park with its old chestnut trees. The church had once been part of the park but had its own plot and drive now. The House still crowned the knoll; its yew walk, the lawns and walled kitchen garden could be seen from the Downs with the stables behind; they had a cupola with a clock and, above the hay loft, a weathercock that, in sunshine, glinted for miles. An avenue of lime trees led to the tall gates where Nat lived alone in the lodge.
(From *The Diddakoi* by Rumer Godden)

Ask your teacher for activity sheet **5.2c** which has a map of the village of Amberhurst. Use the information in the passage to help you identify the following locations on your map. Label your map carefully.

a) The Cuthberts' house
b) The post office
c) The church
d) The common
e) The Council estate
f) The school
g) Miss Brooke's cottage
h) Amberhurst woods
i) The House
j) The stables
k) Nat's lodge
l) The garage

Now use your completed map to give someone detailed directions from:
a) The Cuthberts' house to the church.
b) The Council estate to the lodge.
c) Miss Brooke's house to the garage.
d) The Cuthberts' house to the school.

Writing

Journeys aren't always great, exciting adventures. We all make journeys every day: a journey to school, to the shops, to relatives, etc.

Write an illustrated account of a journey you have made. If you prefer you may write your account as a booklet with the title *Journey to* . . . A little library of *Journey* booklets could then be assembled by your group.

The Story of Our Language

The story of how English developed is fascinating. We will begin with the invasion of Britain by the Angles, Saxons and Jutes in the fifth century A.D.

The Angles, Saxons and Jutes

These invaders came from the shores of what is now known as Holland, Germany and Denmark. They brought with them their language, *Englisc*.

This language was very different from the English of today, but many of its words still survive: *the, you, is, day, night, earth, heaven, light*, for example.

When Saxon words were written down they looked different from our modern spellings. What do you think these words are: *cnif, forgyf, camb, mann, hus*?

Where the Saxons settled they gave their new homes Saxon names with endings such as *-ton* (a place surrounded by a hedge or palisade), *-ham* (village or homestead) and *-den* (valley). Look at a map of Britain and make a list of the place names you find with these endings.

Latin

When St. Augustine came in 597 he brought the Latin language with him and gave us such words as *altar, priest, psalm, hymn, monk* and *abbot*. Latin had been spoken in Britain before the Saxon invasion, when Roman legions occupied this distant outpost of their empire, but its use ended with their withdrawal. Evidence of the occupation can still be seen in some place names. The Latin word *castrum* for a camp or fortified place shows in names such as Doncaster. Sometimes it was changed to *-chester*, as in Dorchester and Winchester. Look for more such names on your map, and make a list of them.

Vikings

The first Viking raiders appeared on the coasts of Britain in 787. Over the next century they began to settle. Place name endings which show Viking origin are *-thorpe* (Danish) and *-thwaite* (Norwegian) meaning farm or settlement, *-wick* (dwelling or farm), *-toft* (a plot of land), and *-by* (from the Danish word "byr" meaning a settlement or town). Whitby and Grimsby are examples of the *-by* ending. Look for these on a map. Does their location tell you anything about the Vikings? Make a list of place names with Viking endings.

The Vikings gave many new words to our language. Here are some examples:
— husband from the Danish words *hus* (house) and *bondi* (a person who lived there). Gradually this came to mean a married man who was master of the house.
— awkward from *awk* meaning the wrong way.
— scale from *scal* meaning bowl. Can you explain how this came to have its modern meaning?

Alfred the Great

Before the Viking invasion scholars wrote and read books in Latin, the language of the Church, but as the Vikings sacked and plundered the monasteries, there were fewer and fewer people able to read them. With the help of some of the remaining Latin scholars, King Alfred translated many of these books into English. Try to find the titles of some of them.

The Normans

The Norman invasion of Britain changed our language for ever. Norman French took over as the language of government and law, and English ceased to be a written language for six generations.

New words passed into the language, e.g. bailiff, perjury, mortgage, reward, chancelor, nobility. *Curfew* comes from the French *couvre-feu* (cover fire) which was a Norman law forcing people to be indoors with fires extinguished by a certain time in the evening. Parlour (from *parler* — to speak) comes from the room in a monastery where monks were allowed to speak. What connection do you think the word *parler* has with the word *parliament*?

Sometimes new words came into the language alongside older words, giving us the shades of meaning which make English such a rich language. Alongside the old Saxon words swine, sheep and ox, came the Norman work pork (*porc*), mutton (*mouton*), and beef (*boeuf*). Can you explain the difference in meaning between the Saxon and Norman words?

The Saxon word for *royal* was *kingly* from king, or cyning. The Normans brought us *royal* as well as *regal* and *sovereign*.

Write a sentence to show the difference in meaning for each word in these groups: **a)** rise, mount, ascend; **b)** ask, question, interrogate.

Middle English

When people came to write again in English it was so very different from Old English that it is now referred to as Middle English. Geoffrey Chaucer's great work, *The Canterbury Tales,* shows how rich the language had become.

New English

Our language continued to change and grow as travellers and explorers brought back new words from other lands. William Shakespeare used many of them in his plays. From Spanish and Portuguese came *potato, tobacco* and *banana;* from French we got *chocolate, cabinet, rabbit, genteel, nephew, niece* and *aunt.* From Italian came *balcony, corridor, colonnade* and *opera.* From Arabic came *algebra, alcohol, sugar, orange* and *sherbet.*

Can you match these English words with their foreign counterparts? Write them in three columns: *English Word, Foreign Word, Language of Origin.* The first example is done for you.

English		Spanish	French	Dutch	Arabic
falcon	waggon	canibales	boucle	jacht	quitar
landscape	cotton	mosca	faucon	landschap	balusi
guitar	mosquito	el lagarto	couvrir	wagen	sukkar
cover	blouse				qutan
yacht	orange				naranj
sugar	buckle				
cannibals	alligator				

English Word	Foreign Word	Language of Origin
falcon	faucon	French

English is a living language and changes wherever it is used. In Unit 5 we will look at these changes in more detail.

Around the World

Countries and their People

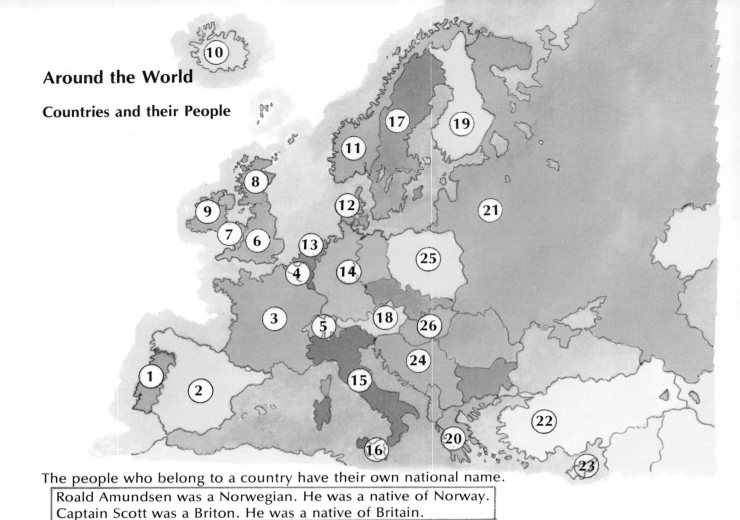

The people who belong to a country have their own national name.

> Roald Amundsen was a Norwegian. He was a native of Norway.
> Captain Scott was a Briton. He was a native of Britain.

Use an atlas to help you match these people to their countries. The first has been done for you.

a) Norwegian   *Norway 11*
b) German
c) Greek
d) Cypriot
e) Irish
f) Swede
g) Dane
h) Belgian
i) Scot

j) French
k) Pole
l) Turk
m) Italian
n) Sicilian
o) Hungarian
p) Austrian
q) Portuguese
r) Russian

s) English
t) Yugoslav
u) Dutch
v) Icelander
w) Finn
x) Welsh
y) Swiss
z) Spaniard

The natives of cities or counties sometimes take a name of their own.
  e.g. Moscow — Muscovite

You may need to use a dictionary to help you find out to which cities or counties these people belong.

Sir, if a man from Moscow is a Muscovite is a man from Paris a Parasite?

a) Parisian
b) Venetian
c) Roman
d) Athenian
e) Liverpudlian

f) Northumbrian
g) Aberdonian
h) Cornish
i) Neapolitan
j) Mancunian

k) Glaswegian
l) Oxonian
m) Lancastrian
n) Cantabrian
o) Devonian

To learn more about countries and their people ask your teacher for activity sheet **5.2e**.

Limericks

There was a young lady of Riga
Who went for a ride on a tiger;
They finished the ride
With the lady inside,
And a smile on the face of the tiger.

There was a young man from Leeds,
He swallowed a packet of seeds;
Flowers grew on his head
But the poor man just said,
"Well, flowers are better than weeds!"

These are a very popular form of verse called limericks. Look closely at the rhyme pattern. The first, second and last line all rhyme, as do the third and fourth. This A A B B A rhyming pattern is traditional in limericks. The first line pattern is traditional too, usually beginning:

"There was a young/old _____ of _____"

Try writing some "Round the World" limericks for yourself.

Here is another type of verse you might like to try.
Look at these photographs, taken from all over the world. Look at them closely. Do they remind you of anything?

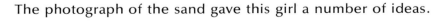

The photograph of the sand gave this girl a number of ideas.

Sand
It looks like the marks of a thousand snakes slithering along,
Or the footprint of a giant's training shoe.
It is sea turned to sand, its waves stilled,
Looking like a range of brownish hills viewed from the air.
It is sand: yellow, wet, wave-moulded sand.

Time Quest

The famous time traveller Hiram K. Cunningham has disappeared in Ancient Egypt. Rumours reach you that he is a prisoner of the Pharoah, and will not be released until he has solved a particularly difficult problem. This he has been unable to do. You set off in your time machine to find and rescue him, arriving at a village near the River Nile.

Problem 1: Who is Your Guide?

Your first problem is to find a guide and a bearer to carry your pack of food, water and valuables.

In the village there are three men on trial for theft, but only one is guilty. The village headman tells you the two innocent men will be your guide and bearer. After listening to their pleas he makes his judgement.

To Hori he says, "If and only if the other two receive the same judgement will you be imprisoned."

To Mosi he says, "If and only if the other two receive the same judgement will you become guide."

To Amon he says, "If and only if the other two receive a different judgement will you become the bearer."

"Here is my judgement: one of you is to be imprisoned, one is to be the guide and the third is to be the bearer."

Who is your guide and who is your bearer? Explain how you solved the problem.

Problem 2: Crossing the Nile

There is a boatman willing to take you across the Nile, but his boat will carry only two people, or one person and your travel pack.

You must never leave the pack unattended at any time, and Hori is the only one you can trust. He tells you it is dangerous for you to be alone on either bank, but you will be safe with the boatman. Only you and the boatmen can sail the boat. Explain how you all get safely across.

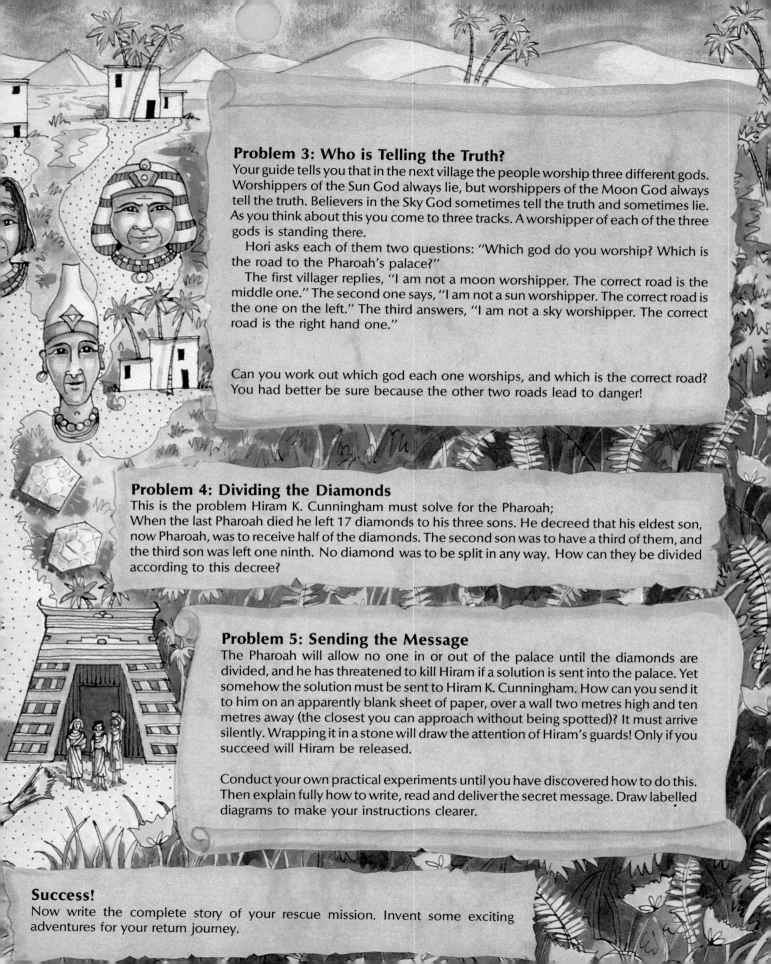

Problem 3: Who is Telling the Truth?

Your guide tells you that in the next village the people worship three different gods. Worshippers of the Sun God always lie, but worshippers of the Moon God always tell the truth. Believers in the Sky God sometimes tell the truth and sometimes lie. As you think about this you come to three tracks. A worshipper of each of the three gods is standing there.

Hori asks each of them two questions: "Which god do you worship? Which is the road to the Pharoah's palace?"

The first villager replies, "I am not a moon worshipper. The correct road is the middle one." The second one says, "I am not a sun worshipper. The correct road is the one on the left." The third answers, "I am not a sky worshipper. The correct road is the right hand one."

Can you work out which god each one worships, and which is the correct road? You had better be sure because the other two roads lead to danger!

Problem 4: Dividing the Diamonds

This is the problem Hiram K. Cunningham must solve for the Pharoah;
When the last Pharoah died he left 17 diamonds to his three sons. He decreed that his eldest son, now Pharoah, was to receive half of the diamonds. The second son was to have a third of them, and the third son was left one ninth. No diamond was to be split in any way. How can they be divided according to this decree?

Problem 5: Sending the Message

The Pharoah will allow no one in or out of the palace until the diamonds are divided, and he has threatened to kill Hiram if a solution is sent into the palace. Yet somehow the solution must be sent to Hiram K. Cunningham. How can you send it to him on an apparently blank sheet of paper, over a wall two metres high and ten metres away (the closest you can approach without being spotted)? It must arrive silently. Wrapping it in a stone will draw the attention of Hiram's guards! Only if you succeed will Hiram be released.

Conduct your own practical experiments until you have discovered how to do this. Then explain fully how to write, read and deliver the secret message. Draw labelled diagrams to make your instructions clearer.

Success!

Now write the complete story of your rescue mission. Invent some exciting adventures for your return journey.

Holidays — What is the Truth?

EXCLUSIVE HOLIDAYS PASICI APARTMENTS

It is our great pleasure to be able to offer you for your "Exclusive" holiday, the recently-built Pasici Apartments.

In these delightful self-catering apartments you will feel right at the centre of things for Pasici is very close to all amenities and within walking distance of the beach. As well as offering awe-inspiring views from the balconies, each apartment affords luxury accommodation other tour operators would find hard to match. A typical apartment here consists of an "all mod cons" kitchen area, superbly furnished dining area and boasts three sumptuous bedrooms. Adjoining each apartment is a neat well-fitted bathroom with shower.

All apartments are regularly cleaned by our highly efficient and well-trained staff, leaving you free to relax and enjoy your "Exclusive" holiday.

Pasici Apartment are in the perfect location for those of you who like to explore the local countryside. For the sun-seekers there is our exclusive sun terrace and private swimming pool.

(For prices and supplements see p107.)

The McGrath family have spent their summer holiday at the Pasici Apartments. Read the brochure which tempted them to go, and then their reactions to the actual apartments.

1   Read the brochure description above carefully and then draw your own "photographs" of the holiday you might expect to have.

2   Look at the complaints of the McGrath family on the opposite page and the photographs they took. Write about what would really happen to you if you were to spend a holiday there. Add "photographs" of your own.

3   Imagine you are one of the McGrath family. Write a letter of complaint to the travel company asking for compensation.

Complaints

Pasici is very close to all amenities

Highly efficient and well-trained - Says who?

A very private and exclusive expensive swimming pool!

Walking distance to the beach? True, but you're too tired to do anything once you're there!

Dad: "Recently built," the brochure said. They were still putting windows and doors in when we arrived!

Girl: We chose Pasici because it had a private pool. We thought it was free, but we had to pay a lot extra to use it. So we didn't.

Mum: I quite liked the idea of the adjoining bathroom, but when we got there we found the bathroom joined *two* apartments, so we were forced to share. That's not the impression the brochure gave me.

Boy: The brochure wasn't wrong when it said we'd be right in the heart of things. What the picture didn't show was that our apartment was built on top of a late night disco. We just couldn't sleep.

1. Read the brochure again. How does it make the apartments seem attractive?
2. Pick out any misleading words and phrases. Is there anything in the brochure's description that is actually untrue?
3. Write an honest description of this holiday location.
4. Read through your description. Do you think your description would make anyone want to go there? Is there any way you can make the apartments seem more attractive without misleading people?

Things to do
1. Look at holiday brochures. Try to pick out words and phrases which make places sound attractive. Look at the photographs. How do they make the place appear interesting and exciting?
2. If you still have brochures for a holiday you have been on, read through the description again. Is it truthful? Is there anything misleading? Did you have the sort of holiday you expected? Write an accurate description based on *your* experiences.

29

Choosing a Holiday

A Read this holiday brochure carefully, paying particular attention to the description of the holiday resort of Bodrum.
Now look at this tree diagram.
Copy the diagram into your book and use the brochure to help you fill in the missing details.

Istanbul

Istanbul is a city of dreams, where East meets West and ancient splendour exists alongside a thriving, vibrant, noisy, exciting and beautiful modern-day city. Here, in the centre of Roman, Ottoman and Byzantine Empires, with the city skyline dominated by minarets, you know you are somewhere different — you have arrived at the gateway to Asia.

No other city can have quite so much to offer its visitors: museums, mosques, the famous Topkapi palace, Scutari — the hospital made famous by Florence Nightingale — and the Grand Oriental Bazaar with over 5 000 shops.

Along the Bosporus, on which this noble city stands, are many colourful fishing villages. No visitor should miss the opportunity of a trip along its shores in a traditional "gulet", with perhaps a freshly caught sea-food lunch prepared at one of the "lokantas" on a nearby island.

Istanbul can also offer you a dazzling and varied nightlife. As well as the wide variety of first-class restaurants that reflect the city's cosmopolitan nature, Istanbul also offers discotheques, casinos and nightclubs where you can discover belly-dancing — the age-old seduction of the East.

Excursions are available including the grand Tour of Istanbul, the Princess Islands Tour and the Bosporus and Asia Tour.

Accommodation in Istanbul tends to be in small hotels. Villas are available, but can be found only outside the city area.

Turkey

Turkey is a country of beauty and contrasts, not just a place to visit, but the rare experience of a lifetime — a glorious amalgam of ancient and modern, blended into one irresistible country. In which other country, only 3½ hours from London, can you find such perfect ingredients for a holiday recipe to suit and surprise all tastes?

Reflecting the contrasting lifestyles that Turkey has to offer, let us look at two very different resorts: Bodrum and Istanbul.

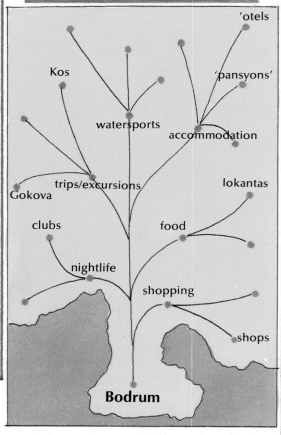

Bodrum

A beautiful medieval castle built by the Knights of St. John guards the entrance to Bodrum Harbour. The town itself is full of whitewashed "sugar cube" houses, while down around the harbour gulets — traditional Turkish wooden sailing boats — jostle with yachts and fishing craft. Bodrum is known as the centre for watersports in Turkey; snorkelling, windsurfing and waterskiing are all widely available here, with excellent tuition. Bodrum is very much a fun place to be, and there are plenty of bars and excellent restaurants.

For those seeking more relaxing pursuits, cruise boats can take you on leisurely trips down the coast to the bay of Gokova, Marmaris or even the Greek island of Kos.

Thursdays and Fridays away from the water give you the opportunity to experience a real Turkish bazaar, when local farmers and tradesmen bring their fresh produce and wares. On other days Bodrum boasts a fine array of shops selling everything from fresh fruit, cheeses and aromatic herbs and spices to carpets, shoes, clothing, and souvenirs.

By night, as the multi-coloured floodlights of the castle spill over the calm waters of the bay, Bodrum's other personality takes over. Bars and "lokantas" cater for every taste with music of western and eastern origins. Discos encourage the energetic, whilst belly dancers in local clubs amaze the onlookers.

Day or night, Bodrum has it all; a fun-loving town you'll want to return to again and again.

Accommodation in the town is as varied as its lifestyle: villas, apartments, "pansyons" and "otels" are all readily available.

B Read the description of Istanbul carefully. Make your own tree diagram to show the facilities it has to offer. You may use the above diagram as a model, or you can make up your own headings.

C 1 Which resort offers most facilities? Give details in your answer.
2 Which resort would you prefer? Give reasons for your answer.
3 Write a postcard from your chosen resort saying what you have been doing.

Imagine that you and your family have decided to book a two week holiday in Istanbul. The prices for full board hotel accommodation and flight information are given here.

PRICES PER PERSON INCLUDING ALL AIRPORT CHARGES DEPARTURES ON OR BETWEEN															
Hotel	Holiday Code	No of Nights	28 Apr-04 May	05 May-23 May	24 May-31 May	01 Jun-20 Jun	21 Jun-03 Jul	04 Jul-15 Jul	16 Jul-15 Aug	16 Aug-23 Aug	24 Aug-29 Aug	30 Aug-12 Sep	13 Sep-03 Oct	04 Oct-23 Oct	Extra Week
Istanbul Manzara ★★	TIM2	7	232	225	256	249	271	283	299	293	279	269	251	227	49
		14	291	299	348	337	379	389	409	399	375	365	321	289	
Istanbul Akman ★★★	TIA2	7	240	228	268	258	288	294	301	304	294	286	260	230	60
		14	300	295	346	358	395	404	414	418	380	374	352	300	
Child Reductions			Half Price	25% off	Half Price	25% off			20% off			25% off		Half Price	FREE

FLIGHT INFORMATION						
Airport	Supplement	First Dept	Last Dept	Flight Day	Dept Time	Return Time
Gatwick	NIL	28 Apr	23 Oct	Fri	0700	1215
Gatwick	£6	05 May	03 Oct	Tues	0710	1340
Stanstead	£6	28 Apr	23 Oct	Fri	1000	1515
Birmingham	£15	28 Apr	23 Oct	Fri	1600	1415
Manchester	£18	05 May	03 Oct	Tues	0730	1345
Manchester	£15	28 Apr	23 Oct	Fri	1700	2255

Flight timings
Gatwick — Dalaman Airport, 3hrs 15mins
Stanstead — Dalaman Airport, 3hrs 20mins
Birmingham — Dalaman Airport, 3hrs 30mins
Manchester — Dalaman Airport, 3hrs 45mins

Your holiday party will consist of two adults and two children. Look at the holiday information carefully and then use it to answer these questions.

1 At what time of year is it cheapest to go on holiday? Can you think why this should be?
2 Why does it cost more to fly from certain British airports?
3 What would be the cost of your holiday if you stayed for seven nights at the Manzara Hotel, departing from Stanstead on May 1st? (Don't forget the child reductions.)
4 How much more expensive would this same holiday be if you were to stay at the Akman Hotel?
5 How much would it cost your family to spend three weeks at the Akman Hotel, departing from Gatwick on Tuesday, August 27th?
6 Imagine your holiday party is setting out from Manchester Airport on Friday, 9th May to spend seven days at the Hotel Manzara. Calculate how much this would cost.

Now ask your teacher for the holiday booking form on activity sheet 5.2f.
Fill in all the necessary details.

Travelling

America

Jobs
Find out about people who make journeys as part of their job: taxi drivers, airline pilots, sailors, bus and train drivers, etc. The Careers Information Service may provide you with posters and leaflets.

FRANCE

MEXICO

Television Commercial
Prepare a TV commercial for your school holiday centre.
Interview "satisfied customers", etc.

CHINA

Graphs
Make a graph to show the different countries your group has visited. Which is the most popular? Why?

australia

DENMA

Guidebooks
Write a guidebook for tourists who visit your local area. Try to present the area in the best possible light. Then write an alternative guidebook which gives a realistic assessment.

JAPAN

India

EGYPT

Round the World
Use a world map to plan a route for a world tour. Write a story to describe your tour. Use travel brochures and reference books to add realism to your account. Draw pictures to illustrate your adventures.

School Holiday Centre
Imagine your school is to be turned into a holiday centre during the holidays. Design a holiday brochure to describe the accommodation and facilities your school has to offer, and what it will cost.

IRELAND

ICELAND

The North Pole
Find out about the conquest of the North Pole. Who was the first to reach it? When? How? Draw a map of the Arctic showing the routes of the early explorers.

GERMANY

AFRICA

Pilgrimages

CANADA

People once made pilgrimages to Canterbury: Chaucer's "Canterbury Tales" is about such a pilgrimage. Muslims make pilgrimages to Mecca. Find out why they go.

Time Zones
If you travel round the world you will cross different time zones. Find out what they are and how they work.
What is G.M.T.?
If it is 12.00 noon G.M.T., what time will it be in these places?
a) New York b) Sydney c) Moscow
d) Tokyo e) Cairo f) Delhi

ITALY

Passports
If you are travelling abroad you will need a passport. Make one of your own with either a self-portrait or a real photograph. Don't forget to include information such as date of birth, height, weight, distinguishing features, etc.

Travel Agency
Set up a travel agency in your classroom with posters, brochures and information on popular resorts, both at home and abroad.

PERU

Thai

AUSTRIA

Story Writing
Choose one of these titles and write an illustrated story.
A Journey of a Lifetime
Journey Into Space
To the Depths of the Ocean
A Journey to the Heart of the Earth
Mystery Tour
My Dream Holiday

UNIT 3 The Media

When we refer to the media we usually mean newspapers, television and radio. These offer information and entertainment, but quite often they attempt to persuade us in some way. Advertisements are an obvious example of persuasion, but other ways are used too, as you will discover in this unit.

To think and talk about

A The Media

1 Think about television. Which programmes offer entertainment? Which give information? In what ways does television attempt to persuade us?
2 Is this equally true of radio?
3 Look at two different daily newspapers. How much space do they devote to information, to entertainment and to advertisements? Are the proportions the same in each newspaper? Can you give a reason for this?

B News

1 What is news? Make a list of events which you think would be news. Can you think of events which a newspaper would not consider worth reporting? Why is this?
2 Try to find examples of the following kinds of news: personal, local, national and international.
3 Where does news come from? How does a newspaper find its news?
4 Apart from newspapers, in what other ways can news be communicated to its audience?

An Audience Survey

Every news editor needs to know who his audience is, and what interests them. Find out for yourself the kinds of news which interest different people.

Begin with your class. Plan a questionnaire to find out the answers to these questions:

How many read newspapers? Which ones do they read? Do they read newspapers written especially for children? Which do they prefer? Can they say why?

How many watch news on television, or listen to it on the radio?

Which medium do they prefer? Why?

Which news items interest them most? Which least?

When you have conducted your survey decide on the best way to present your findings, e.g. a graph, a chart, etc.

Use the same questionnaire to survey: a) children of a different age range, b) your family. Compare and discuss the results.

A Newspaper Survey

Collect as many different national newspapers as you can for a particular day.

Share out the papers so that each can be studied by a small group. Find answers to the following questions:

1 Is the paper a broadsheet or a tabloid? (The page size of a tabloid is half that of a broadsheet.)
2 How many stories are there on the front page?
3 How much of the front page is taken up by the main headline?
4 Which stories does the paper treat as the most important? How do you know?

5 What proportion of space is taken by
   a) text? b) pictures? c) advertisements?
   Present your findings as a pie chart.

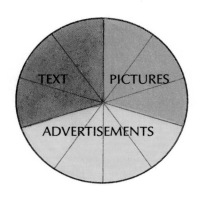

6 How much space is taken by non-news items,
   e.g. cartoons, horoscopes, recipes, letters,
   TV and radio schedules, etc.? Show this
   proportion in a second pie chart.

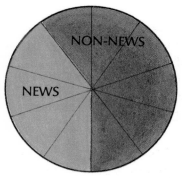

7 Does the layout of the newspaper make you want to read it? Can you say why?
8 Can you say who the paper is intended to interest? What makes you think so?

Compare the results of your survey with those of the other groups. Look particularly for answers to these questions:

1 Do the papers choose the same main story? Why do you think this is? How many different main stories are there?
2 Does any paper have a scoop (an important story that the other papers have failed to cover)?
3 Are the five most important stories in one paper covered in all the others? Are the stories given the same degree of importance?
4 Are there stories which are reported in some papers, but not covered in the others? Why do you think this is?
5 Look at the stories which appear in more than one paper. Are these reported differently in different papers? Explain how they are different. Can you think of any reason for this?

READ ALL ABOUT IT!

NEXT TIME you chew or suck your pen top — THINK! It's a startling fact that in Britain one child every year dies from inhaling a pen top! It just gets stuck in the windpipe and stops you breathing. If you don't need the top then throw it away before an accident happens.

The Royal Society for the Prevention of Accidents(RoSPA) warns children about other things that spell DANGER! Marbles, coins, stones, paper clips and even bits of paper. Don't think that they're too small to block your throat.

STOP PRESS: A Leicester schoolboy, Billy Walker, tragically died last week after choking on a pen top.

A LITTLE girl got in a jam when she went for a bite to eat with her mum in a Failsworth supermarket cafe.

The three-year-old stuck fast, trapped by her leg between two seats, and despite desperate efforts by restaurant staff, could not be moved.

Manageress of Morrisons restaurant in Poplar Street, Mrs Jill Hampson said she tried to pull the unfortunate youngster free but to no avail.

Eventually firemen were called to the scene and the by now tearful girl was freed within minutes.

"The poor little girl thought she was stuck there forever," said Jill.

WHEN it comes to fighting crime against the elderly, 30 Oldham schoolchildren are top of the class!

Now, the ideas which won class 2GP, of St Augustine of Canterbury RC Secondary School, first prize in an Oldham probation service competition, could soon be put into operation by Greater Manchester Police.

Schools had to chose an area of crime and then come up with ideas to beat the problem.

The St Augustine children, who were all 12-year-olds at the time, concentrated on the elderly — who they saw as society's most vulnerable group.

"The class went out into the community interviewing pensioners about their fears," said teacher Mrs Maureen Quinn.

"Then they came up with ideas and suggestions to beat the criminals."

'Raise money for those who raised you' and 'If in doubt lock them out' were just two of the slogans used by the second-year pupils.

They also produced a booklet — 'The 12 Golden Rules for the Elderly' — and two ideas which could soon be put into force:

● Awarding grants to the elderly to make their homes secure.

● Dividing towns into zones so that every elderly person has a public building they could contact if they needed help.

The children's efforts won their school a TV and video as well as praise from their teachers.

SCHOOLBOY Christopher Wilson is lucky to be alive after sleepwalking from a moving train.

Christopher, 16, stepped out as the train pulled in to Andover, Hants, then tumbled down a 30ft embankment.

The teenager was travelling from London, where he lives with his father, to his school near Andover.

A police spokesman said yesterday Christopher narrowly missed falling onto a busy road. "He was saved by the embankment. I dread to think what might have happened—especially as it was rush-hour."

Lizardman leaps into US folklore

SIGHTINGS of a monster lizard from the swamp have struck terror in a small community in South Carolina, *writes Stephen Milligan.*

The scare began when Christopher Davis, a young driver, claimed he had been attacked by a scaly creature that was green, wet, three-fingered, red-eyed and 7ft tall. Davis said the monster chased his car at speeds up to 40mph and jumped on his roof.

The monster apparently appeared from the nearby Scape Ore swamp. Two police officers found enormous footprints a mile away.

A state biologist suggested that Davis probably saw a drunk who had got out of a muddy ditch. And the local sheriff believes the monster was a bear and that the tracks were made by a prankster.

But the story has been widely believed and there have been other sightings. Last week a local couple reported that their car had been "chewed up" in their garage one night.

Since then, some 70 hunters have been trying to trap the monster, dubbed Lizardman.

On Friday morning, a motorist claimed that he had shot Lizardman but had failed to kill it. He handed police a tissue which he said was stained with the monster's blood.

The sheriff sent two deputies to the scene of the shooting but found no trace of the

monster. A local radio station has offered a reward of $1m to anybody who can capture Lizardman alive or dead.

Erik Beckjord, a leading "monsterologist", says Lizardman may be a "skunk ape", a creature said to have been sighted in woods and swamps across America for the past 30 years.

Other giant creatures which are said to be stalking the countryside include the Jersey Devil, which has a horse's face and a kangaroo's body and emits a piercing howl, and the Dover Demon, an orange animal with a head shaped like the figure eight, which lives in Massachusetts.

They have one common feature: they attract tourists.

FLIGHTS from airports all over Britain were delayed yesterday after the country's main air traffic control computer suddenly and spectacularly broke down.

Air traffic controllers at West Drayton centre, which co-ordinates flights to and from Europe as well as internal traffic, were forced to track flights by hand for nearly five hours during one of the busiest weekends of the year.

A Civil Aviation Authority spokesman said that "in the interests of safety" controllers had to impose extra restrictions on the number of flights. "Obviously everything is slowed down and controllers can handle less traffic," he said.

A DOG was swallowed by a giant pike in a Russian river, recently. A fisherman caught the 5ft 8inches fish, cut it open, and the dog squeezed out barking happily.

TWO BRAVE British girls took 26 hours off the world record of the toughest run. Last week Allison Wright, 21, and Helen Diamantes, 22, ran the 164 mile journey from the foot of Mount Everest to Katmandu in 3 days and 10 hours!

(5.3f)

About the News Cuttings

1 Search Reading

Use search reading to find the answers to the questions below.

First scan the headlines and topic sentences to find the correct report. The topic sentence tells us what the report is about. It is usually the first sentence in the report.

Secondly skim through the report until you find the information you need.

Finally read that part of the report carefully.

a) What were the names of the two British girls who ran 164 miles?
b) List five objects you are warned not to chew or suck.
c) What happened to Christopher Wilson?
d) Why were airport flights delayed?
e) What extraordinary thing happened to a dog in Russia?
f) Who rescued a little girl in a supermarket?
g) What ideas did schoolchildren have for fighting crime?
h) What was the cause of the tragedy on the Ganges River?
i) Give two possible explanations for the sighting of the lizardman. What do you think the writer of the article thinks about these sightings?

300 drown as steamer sinks

NEW DELHI: Some 300 people are feared drowned after an overcrowded steamer capsized yesterday in the Ganges River in eastern India's Bihar state.

Rescue services were being rushed to the scene of the disaster, which occurred on the rain-swollen Ganges about 12 miles from Katihar city in the remote north of the state.

The large steamer was packed with Hindu pilgrims travelling to Deoghar, Bihar's holiest Hindu town where thousands of devotees flock during the summer monsoon for an annual religious celebration. *(AFP)*

2 Find one example of each of the following kinds of news:
   a) local news
   b) national news
   c) international news
   d) good news
   e) bad news
   f) news aimed at children
Write the topic sentence of each one.

3 Headlines

Two of the reports have headlines. Read them carefully and you will notice the following important points:

a) Headlines are written in the present tense, e.g. "300 drown as steamer sinks", even though the reports themselves are written in the past tense.
b) Words such as "a" or "the" are left out.
c) Headlines need to be short, no more than six words, but should say what the report is about.
d) Headlines often use alliteration (words beginning with the same sound) to catch attention, e.g. "Lizardman leaps into US folklore".

The headlines of the remaining articles have been left off. Use the rules above to write a headline for each one.

4 a) If you were the editor of a newspaper for children, which *five* reports do you think would most interest your readers? List them in the order of their importance.
   b) Do the same for a newspaper aimed at adults.
   c) Which stories would appear in only one of the papers? Can you explain this?

5 One of the articles has the letters AFP at the end. This stands for "Agence France Press". Why do you think the letters are there?

6 Make up six questions of your own about the reports on this page. Ask a friend to find the answers.

Reporting

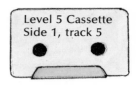
To think and talk about

Listen to this track on the listening skills tape. It features a traditional tale called *News* and a poem based on another tale, *The Blindmen and the Elephant*.

News
1 Did you find the story sad, funny or both? How has the writer made you feel that way?
2 Do you think a newspaper report would begin with the death of the magpie? How do you think it would begin? Give a reason for your answer.
3 Think of a good headline for such a newspaper report.

The Blindmen and the Elephant
1 Why does each person give a different description of the elephant?
2 How accurate do you think each description is?
3 How would it be possible to get a full and accurate description?

Points of View
The Blindmen and the Elephant shows that a situation can be interpreted differently by different people. Each one sees it from his own point of view.

This makes a reporter's job difficult. He has to report events as accurately as he can, but he might not always discover *all* the facts, and sometimes he may see events from a misleading viewpoint.

Look at these two stories. Each reporter believes he has written a factual report of the events.

Skinhead Stones Picnickers

A quiet picnic came to a violent end today as a mother and daughter were attacked by a youth.

Mrs. Vivienne Driscoll and daughter Beverley, 9, had stopped for a picnic lunch on Starbury Hill.

"It was a lovely day," said Mrs. Driscoll later. "We were just relaxing after a long walk when a stone crashed inches away from where we were sitting. I turned round to see a skinhead waving his arms threateningly and screaming 'Get away!'"

As Mrs. Driscoll rose to her feet the youth picked up a second stone and hurled it at them.

"I grabbed hold of Beverley's hand, and we just ran," said Mrs. Driscoll angrily.

The area has developed a poor reputation in recent weeks. On Sunday a pensioner was frightened by two youths as he was walking his dog. The police are investigating both incidents.

Youth Saves Couple from Python Attack!

A woman and a girl had the narrowest of escapes today, as a seventeen year old boy saved them from an escaped python.

Young Graham Mathieson of Kingston Avenue was on Starbury Hill collecting insects for a school assignment when he spotted the snake in a hollow, just feet away from where the woman and girl were having a picnic.

"I knew it must be the one that had escaped from Ridley Zoo," Graham told our reporter later. "It was moving close to the woman and girl who had their backs to it. Almost without thinking I threw a stone to distract it. The stone missed, but the woman turned round. I shouted to her to get away, but she seemed too frightened to move, so I threw another stone."

Graham's second stone did the trick. The python slid swiftly back into the hollow as the picnickers ran for their lives.

The snake was later recaptured, none the worse for the experience, but the lucky couple have yet to be found.

1 Explain how the first reporter came to get his story so completely wrong.
2 Write a report combining all the known facts from both accounts.

To think and talk about

1 Can a report ever be completely accurate? What could a reporter do to make his report as accurate as possible? Has he time to do these things?
2 Suppose his editor cut out parts of his report to fit the space available in the paper? What effect might this have on the news story?

Writing a Newspaper Report

In Level 4 we gave these Editors' Guidelines to reporters.
Look for answers to these questions:

> **Who** did it?
> **Where** did it happen?
> **When** did it happen?
> **What** happened?
> **Why** did it happen?
> **How** did it end?

The answers to these questions will help you to find the facts of an event. They will give you a summary of what happened. Keep to these facts when you write your report. Never include your own opinion.

1 Write your own news report about something that has happened in your school or neighbourhood. Use the above Editors' Guidelines to help you. Don't forget to choose a suitable headline.
2 Choose an exciting event from a fiction book you have read recently and write it up as a news story.

The Silly Season

The silly season is when there is a shortage of interesting news. It is then that news editors choose silly or strange stories to interest their readers.

Look again at the news stories on pages 36-37. Which of these might be silly season stories? Give a reason for your answer.

Sometimes ordinary news items are sensationalised. This means making them sound far more exciting than they really are. Look at this example.

> **Pensioner's dash averts tragedy**
> Quick thinking from Fred Hawkins, a Belfield senior citizen, saved a mother-to-be from almost certain injury this morning. Fred saw Mrs. Linda Anfield stumble at the edge of the pavement. Without a thought for his own safety he dashed forward and helped her to regain her balance. Within minutes a juggernaut lorry was thundering past.
> "It was a close one," Fred told our reporter later. Mrs. Anfield is now recovering from the shock at the home of her sister, Mrs. Michelle Dodds.

Writing

1 Write your own sensational newspaper report about a very ordinary incident, such as missing a bus, finding something, being late for school, etc. etc.
2 Imagine the events that gave rise to these headlines. Write a sensational report for one of them.

MERMAID CAUGHT BY NORTH SEA TRAWLER   **Ice lolly shock!**

NEW LAW BANS POP MUSIC   **Mystery bug hits school**

Top scientist's amazing breakthrough   Giant hedgehog scares PM

Direct and Reported Speech

Many newspaper reports tell us what people have said. Sometimes they tell us the actual words spoken, like this:

> "We were relaxing after a walk when a stone crashed inches away from us!" said Mrs. Driscoll.

This is known as *direct speech*. The actual words spoken are written inside speech marks.
At other times what people have said is reported without quoting their exact words, like this:

> Mrs. Driscoll said that they were relaxing after a walk when a stone crashed inches away from them.

This is called *reported speech*. There are no speech marks because the actual words spoken are not given.

A   Change these sentences to *reported speech*.
Begin like this:

> Sue said that when she leaves school . . .

When I leave school I want to be an air hostess.

I'm afraid of flying.

I've been on hundreds of flights, and I've enjoyed every one!

My Dad flies to France nearly every month.

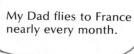

Sue   **James Wilson**   **Freddie Kirkpatrick**   **Kevin**

B Change these sentences to *direct speech*.

1 The policeman asked the boy where he was going.
2 Ian said he could not wait for the start of the holidays.
3 Mother told me she was going to buy a new coat.
4 The teacher told John that his work was the best he had ever done.
5 The driver asked to be directed to the nearest car park.
6 Jessica said she was tired of reading and wanted to go shopping.
7 He said that an inspection of the premises had already taken place.
8 Ranjit asked Ben for help with his homework.
9 Wilson remarked that two hours was rather a long time for such a short walk.
10 Mr. Slocum questioned him on the condition of the fire extinguishers.

C 1 Think of a suitable title for this picture.
   2 Write two versions of what you think the people are saying,
       first as *direct speech* and then as *reported speech*.

D Write this conversation in *reported speech*.

Danny: Do gorillas have long arms and green hair?
Sarah: They don't have green hair.
Danny: Do they have three red eyes, long, sharp horns and claws like hooked knives?
Sarah: No they don't.
Danny: In that case I don't think it can be a gorilla.
Sarah: What are you talking about?
Danny: That horrible monster standing just behind you.
Sarah: Aaargh!

E Sonia Keene from *The Daily Echo* is interviewing witnesses. Write her news story so that it contains a mixture of direct and reported speech.

What did you see, Mr. Hughes?

What did you do then?

What happened then, Mrs. Davies?

What happened next?

Was he all right?

Thank you both for your help.

I saw a small boy sitting in the driving seat of a red Ford Escort. He was sounding the horn and laughing.

I went across to tell him to stop, but before I got there the car started to roll down the hill. He must have released the handbrake.

I was just crossing the road at the bottom of the hill when the car came rushing towards me. I leaped out of the way just in time.

The car mounted the pavement and began to roll up a grassy bank. By a miracle it came to a stop. Then the door opened and a little boy jumped out crying.

He was until his mother came. She gave him quite a telling off, I can tell you!

Oil Strike!

Northstar Oil have carried out exploratory drilling in the area around the Wessex village of Oakmead, where they have found vast reserves of oil. The government would like Northstar to extract the oil, but the people of Oakmead think differently.

Newspaper reporters have come to the village to talk to the local people and their M.P., Nicholas Grantly. This is what they are told.

Alfred Mellstock, *retired farm labourer*
At 83 I'm too old to get worked up about something I can do nothing about. They say in ten years everything will be as good as it is today. I'm looking forward to seeing if they're right!

William Stokes, *dairy farmer*
Northstar intend sinking their wells right in the middle of my land. My family have farmed here for nigh on three hundred years. The compensation offer is a sick joke!

Martin Fitzpiers, *TV producer*
We can't stop them by talking. Actions speak louder than words.

Valerie Marshall, *Householder*
I'm very happy living in Oakmead. If I'm forced to move, it won't be easy finding a buyer who wants to live next to an oil well.

Vincent Blythe, *Northstar spokesman*
When the oil is exhausted we undertake to restore the Oakmead landscape completely.

Transcript of a recorded interview with Nicholas Grantly, M.P.

Reporter 1: Are you backing your constituents in their fight against Northstar Oil, Mr. Grantly?

Grantly: Let me assure you that I fully appreciate their anxieties.

Reporter 1: Yet the government, your own party, is in favour of on-shore oil extraction at Oakmead.

Grantly: Yes, that's so. The oil reserves under and around Oakmead village are vast. Northstar have agreed to make the absolute minimum disturbance to the area, and after the estimated ten years life of the field they will completely restore its natural beauty. In the meantime there will be more jobs created in the area, and every man, woman and child in this country will benefit from Oakmead oil. However, I do appreciate the genuine concern of the local people and that is why I have arranged for a full debate on the Northstar project in the Village Hall next Wednesday. I feel absolutely certain that this will result in clearing up misunderstandings on both sides.

Reporter 2: But the villagers say talking has proved to be a waste of time. Northstar are poised to bulldoze their way through the Oakmead pastures as soon as the PM gives them the go-ahead.

Grantly: You underestimate the good sense of my constituents. You must excuse me now, ladies and gentlemen, I have an appointment with the Prime Minister.

Bias

The two news reports are about the same event, but they give their readers very different impressions. They show *bias*. Bias means stating facts in such a way as to influence the way people read or hear them. One newspaper is biased in favour of Northstar Oil, but the other is biased against it.

1 Which newspaper do you think is biased against Northstar Oil? Give reasons for your answer.
2 How does the other paper:
   a) make the demonstrators seem unreasonable?
   b) present its own views of the Northstar project?

This is the news report printed in *The Daily Record*.

The *Wessex Observer* featured this report.

Angry Demo At Northstar Site

There was an angry demonstration by local people yesterday at a Northstar drilling site in Wessex. It was the latest of several such demonstrations in Oakmead village during recent months.

TV producer, Martin Fitzpiers, a very recent Oakmead resident, took a leading role in the demonstration. Fitzpiers, whose current BBC TV series "Firepower" has been severely criticised for excessive violence, stated that the people of Oakmead would fight Northstar. "Actions speak louder than words," he warned. A reply by a spokesman for Northstar was lost in the chants of the crowd.

Northstar completed their oil explorations last May, and have since been awaiting the outcome of a series of meetings with the local people and the government. The Oakmead area has vast reserves of oil, which will be a tremendous boost to Britain's balance of payments, and create up to ninety new jobs. Northstar have already undertaken to restore the natural beauty of the area when the oil runs out in about ten years time.

Not all Oakmead residents object to Northstar's plans. Ms. Valerie Marshall told the *Record* she is happy to live in Oakmead. Alfred Melstock, a retired farm labourer, said he is looking foward to seeing the area re-landscaped.

East Wessex M.P. Nicholas Grantly also spoke at the demonstration. "I do appreciate the genuine concern of the local people," he said later. "That is why I have arranged a full debate on the Northstar project in the Oakmead village hall next Wednesday."

Grantly was confident that the community would come to see the advantages of Oakmead oil. After the demonstration he left Wessex for Downing Street to report the views of his constituents to the Prime Minister.

OAKMEAD OIL PROTEST

The determined farmers and villagers of Oakmead held another peaceful demonstration against Northstar Oil today. They voiced their fears of lost farms, plummeting property values and a devastated environment.

Northstar are awaiting government approval to begin pumping oil in the Oakmead area. At least one farm will be lost if the project goes ahead. The very real fear of the local people is that one of the best loved beauty spots in the south of England will be ruined forever.

Northstar's claim that extensive landscaping would later restore the area, has to be seen against their record in Melset. Fountain Melbury, a once lovely valley, is still scarred two years after Northstar declared its landscaping programme a success.

Farmer William Stokes addressed the rally and explained how he would be forced to sell his family farm. "Northstar intend sinking their wells right in the middle of my land," he said sadly. "My family has lived here for three hundred years." He described the compensation offered by Northstar as a "sick joke."

Miss Valerie Marshall, a teacher at Oakmead Primary, warned of falling property values. "Who wants to live next to an oil well?" she asked.

The most famous Oakmead resident, TV producer Martin Fitzpiers, stressed the importance of the demonstration. "Actions speak louder than words," he said.

Nicholas Grantly, M.P., still appears to believe that the Oakmead community will give in to Northstar. He has arranged yet another talk by Northstar in Oakmead village hall on Wednesday next. Judging by the determination shown this afternoon he is in for a rude awakening.

Selecting Facts

Read the two reports again. Are any important facts left out in either report? Why do you think this has been done?

Writers and speakers often select only the facts which support their point of view. Both newspapers have carefully selected what they have reported about the Oakmead demonstration.

1   List the facts left out by: a)   *The Daily Record.*
                                   b)   *The Wessex Observer.*
2   Look in turn at each fact on your list. Can you explain why it has been omitted?

Distortion

If you read the words spoken by the Oakmead demonstrators you will see that the reporters have not only carefully selected which quotes to use, but in some cases have distorted what has been said.

1   How has *The Daily Record* made the words of Martin Fitzpiers seem like a threat?
2   How has it distorted the views of Valerie Marshall?
3   Alfred Mellstock says he is looking forward to the landscaping of Oakmead. What do you think he really means by this?
4   How well does *The Wessex Observer* report their views?

Writing an Unbiased Report

Write an unbiased report on the Oakmead demonstration:

—   report both sides of the issue fairly
—   include all the relevant facts
—   make accurate quotes from the interviews to show the full range of opinion
—   do not add any opinions of your own

News Editor

A news editor has to select news items for his paper, and to decide which to use for his lead story, i.e. the main story on the front page.

As he does so he has to keep his audience in mind. He must choose stories which will interest his readers, and he must present them in a way they will find informative and enjoyable. If he fails then his readers may stop buying his paper.

Look at these newspapers. Each one has its own special audience.

The Daily Echo is a broadsheet. It has plenty of room on its front page for three or four main stories. Its readers have time to read long reports. They like to see at least one photograph on the front page, but are more interested in reading detailed stories on a wide variety of subjects.

The Morning Post is a tabloid. It usually has just one story on its front page, but often has a second headline for a report on page 2. The headlines are large and exciting. There is always an eye-catching photograph. Because the *Post's* readers have less time to spend reading, the reports are shorter than those of *The Daily Echo*. The most popular reports deal with exciting, funny or unusual events, sport and well-known personalities.

The Young Reporter is a tabloid written especially for readers aged 11-14. There are usually two stories on the front page. Its news editor is always on the lookout for stories about children, or those which he thinks will interest them. Whenever possible he tries to find "good news" stories.

Imagine that your group is the editorial team of either *The Daily Echo, The Morning Post* or *The Young Reporter*.

Your task is to select news items to interest your readers. You will find a range of news stories on side 1, track 6 of Level 5 cassette, and on the special activity sheets headed *News Editor*.

Choose at least six of these items, one of which is to be your lead story. Decide amongst yourselves who is to write each story, and how it should be written to interest your readers.

Presenting your material

You will need to prepare a front page and an inside page. Use sugar paper, cut to the appropriate size, to paste your reports on. Don't forget to think of good headlines. Draw "photographs" to accompany your stories. You may add advertisements, cartoons, etc., if space permits.

A School Newspaper

By now you will have learned enough about newspapers to write one of your own. A school newspaper needs a lot of work and careful planning, but if the work is shared out it can be fun.

Your team will include the editor, several sub-editors, reporters and other writers.

Planning Your Newspaper

1 Content
Decide what should go in your paper, e.g.

class and school news
sports news
photographs
interviews
feature articles
reviews (books, TV programmes, records, plays and concerts)
diary of forthcoming events
readers' letters
advice columns
opinion polls
cartoons
crosswords and puzzles
competitions
advertisements

2 Format
Decide what your paper will look like. Consider these points:
— the size of each page, and how many of them you will need,
— how you will print and duplicate your paper,
— the number of copies you will need,
— a selling price which will be affordable, yet cover costs.

You may decide to have a single copy of the paper and display it on a wall board. This is cheaper to produce, and easier to update, but only a limited number of people can read it at any one time, and no one can take it home.

You will also need to think of a suitable name for your paper.

3 Writing and Editing
Decide who is going to write each item. Each item should be written in rough, ready for editing.

Editing is the job of the editor and sub-editors. They will need to do several things:
— select which items to use
— suggest improvements
— shorten items to fit the paper, or ask for further material
— correct spelling and punctuation
— decide which item to use as the lead story
— write exciting headlines

4 Publishing
Notice how items in a real newspaper are printed in columns. Your articles should also be written in columns, either by hand or by using a word processor.

The items should then be cut up so that various layouts of the finished page may be experimented with. If a more urgent report comes along before the paper is finished you will still have time to re-set your page.

When you are happy with the layout paste the items into position. Copies may then be made using a photocopier. Now fasten your paper together and distribute it to your readers.

News on Television

To think and talk about

A 1 How do you feel when you see television news of war, disaster or death? Can you explain why you feel like this?
   2 How does your family react to such scenes?
   3 Can you explain why such news on television is more disturbing than photographs and reports in newspapers?
   4 Which do you find more disturbing: TV news reports, disaster movies or horror films? Can you say why?

B 1 How is TV news different from news in newspapers or on the radio?
   2 What can TV news show us that newspapers can't?
   3 Can you think of any ways in which newspapers are preferable to TV news?
   4 Record a TV news programme. How many stories does it cover? Which reports feature film or video? Which feature still photographs only? Why do you think this is?
      Are there any live news reports in the programme?
      Look at a newspaper which covers the same day's news. How are the events treated differently in the newspaper? Can you say why this is?

A TV Newsreader's Prompting Device

Newsreaders do not learn their lines as an actor does, but they hardly ever look at a script. What they use instead is a prompting device, which allows them to read their words as they look at the camera. The diagram shows how it works.

   Study it carefully and then write a paragraph explaining in your own words how a prompting device works.

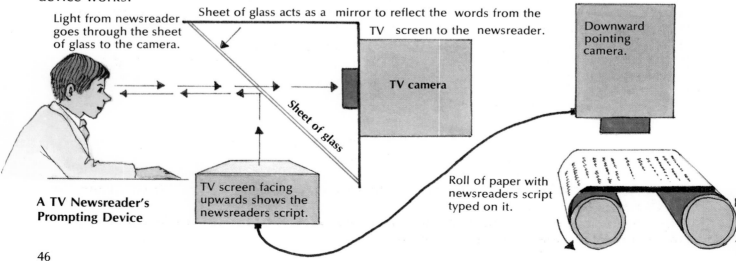

Light from newsreader goes through the sheet of glass to the camera.

Sheet of glass acts as a mirror to reflect the words from the TV screen to the newsreader.

Downward pointing camera.

TV camera

Sheet of glass

TV screen facing upwards shows the newsreaders script.

A TV Newsreader's Prompting Device

Roll of paper with newsreaders script typed on it.

TV Programme Guide

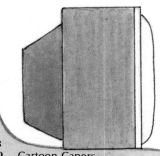

TV 1

5.00 Open Book
The world of children's books with Melanie Hamilton

5.30 Fat Cat
Cartoon series. Tonight Fat Cat bites off more than he can chew!

5.45 Fred'll Fix It
Popular DIY programme. Tonight Fred looks at plumbing

6.00 News Headlines

6.16 Every Good Turn
Situation comedy programme with more yawns than laughs

6.45 Early Knight Line-up
Les Knight talks to a line-up of celebrity guests, including chart toppers Crocodile Mousse

7.15 Take the Money and Run
Basil Hall hosts TV's most popular quiz show.

7.45 Film Night: 18 Carat Cops starring Howie Hopkin and Stella McCoy as New York cops tracking down stolen gold

9.00 Nine O'Clock News with Fiona Reid

9.30-
10.30 Sports Special
Snooker, boxing and highlights of today's soccer action

TV3

5.00 Cartoon Capers

5.30 News at 5.30 with Shireen Shama

5.45 The Trudy McGraw Show
Trudy's mother decides to take driving lessons — with disastrous results!

6.15 Local News

6.45 The Holiday Show
Faith Adams visits Florida, whilst John Gross samples the delights of Cleethorpes and Albania.

7.15 Honeymead Farm
Tina's sudden decision to leave the farm surprises the Pearson family.

8.15 Insight
Andrew Gallagher asks "What is happening to our weather?"

9.00-
10.00 Breakthrough
Episode 2 of this exciting thriller. Reporter Mark Lehman stumbles on something nasty in a quiet seaside town.

1 For how long could you watch cartoons?
2 How many news broadcasts could you watch?
3 If you were able to watch TV between 5.00 and 9.00 with an hour off at a time of your choice, which programmes would you watch? Give reasons for your choice.
4 Which programmes would you watch if you were interested in:
   a) sport? b) current affairs? c) famous people? d) do-it-yourself? e) comedy?
5 Which programmes will these people probably watch?
   a) Jacky likes serials and pop music.
   b) Jason likes action and adventure.
   c) Mrs. Green is a Basil Hall fan, and likes to learn about far away places.
   d) Mr Johnson is a a practical man who likes current affairs programmes.
   e) Miss Armitage likes programmes which make her laugh, and likes to see at least one news bulletin. She will be out of the house from 7.00.
6 What kind of audience might be interested in these programmes?
   a) TV1 at 5.00 b) TV3 at 6.45 c) TV1 at 9.30 d) TV3 at 8.15 e) TV3 at 5.00 f) TV1 at 7.45
7 For each channel try to make a list of programmes under these headings:

children's programmes	news and current affairs
drama serials	instructional programmes
films	comedy
quiz shows	chat shows

For each channel add the times of the programmes in each category, and then compare how much time each channel gives them.

8 The programme guide gives us facts about the programmes, but it also reveals the opinions of the writer. Write down two such opinions.

Give it a Spin!

"And now, Lennie, you have won over three thousand dollars in cash and merchandise and, more important, you have won the chance to spin our Vacation Wheel. How do you feel about that, Lennie?"

"Real good, sir."

"Then join me over here at the Vacation Wheel. Now, Lennie, I don't have to remind you that up there on the wheel are twenty, all-expense paid vacations to places all over the world, do I?"

"No, sir."

"That's twenty, all-expense paid vacations! You can go to Rome, to London, to Paris. You can go to beautiful Hawaii, exotic Mexico or sunny Spain. All in all, there are twenty, wonderful, all-expense paid vacations up there on the wheel. But, Lennie, as you know, there are also what we call our zonk trips. How do you feel about those, Lennie?"

"Well, I hope I don't get one."

"And that's what we're hoping too, aren't we, folks? Hear that applause, Lennie? They're all with you. Now step up close to the Vacation Wheel. That's right. The three zonk trips, as we call them, are here and here and here. Try not to land on them."

"I will, sir."

"All right, put up your hand now, Lennie, right here on the Vacation Wheel, and Lennie, *give it a spin!*"

"Here goes!"

"Good boy! The wheel is spinning, folks. Lennie really gave it a good spin, didn't he? Where do you want to go, Lennie?"

"Any of those places is all right with me."

"Except the zonk places, right?"

"Right."

"It's still spinning, and now it's beginning to slow down. Watch the wheel, folks. Where is Lennie going? To Paris? Rome? London? It's almost stopped. It looks like *Egypt!* No! *Rio!* No! *Oh, no!* Look at that! Lennie, you have landed on number thirteen, one of our zonk trips, and I don't have to tell you what that means."

"It means I'm gong to have to take a zonk trip."

"Right."

"Where?"

"Well, let me look in my zonk envelope. Oh, Lennie."

"What?"

"*Oh,* Lennie."

"What? What is it?"

"*Oh, Lennie!*"

"What? I want to know. What is it?"

"Lennie, you are going to have to spend one full night, all-expense paid, in a *haunted house!*"

(From *The TV Kid* by Betsy Byars)

1 What do you think Lennie has done to have won so much money?
2 What is "merchandise"?
3 Explain in your own words what a zonk trip is.
4 What might the other two zonk trips be?
5 Why do you think the presenter delays in telling Lennie what his zonk trip is?
6 How would you feel if you were Lennie?

Writing
1 Write an account of what you think Lennie's zonk trip will be like.
2 Invent a zonk trip of your own and write an account of your experiences.
3 Describe your idea of a dream holiday.

Reading and Thinking

Think for yourself what the missing words are in this passage. Write one word for each space.

Basil Hall, host of the TV quiz show "Take The Money and Run", smiled into the TV camera, his hand poised over a golden telephone.

"This is the part of our show when we give a lucky viewer a golden opportunity to appear on the show and _____1_____ one of the prizes listed on _____2_____ wheel behind me. Someone out there _____3_____ about to get a call from _____4_____. I am now going to dial _____5_____ number, completely at random, although _____6_____ area code has already been selected. _____7_____ your phone should ring then all _____8_____ have to do is answer "Hello, Basil" and _____9_____ me the password, which today is "Gold". _____10_____ I'm dialling take a look at _____11_____ week's fabulous prizes."

As Basil began to _____12_____ a series of numbers on the golden _____13_____, the prize wheel slowly began to _____14_____ revealing the exciting prizes on offer. The _____15_____ in the studio waited with bated _____16_____, as did millions of viewers sitting at _____17_____. Somewhere at the end of the _____18_____ link a distant telephone began to _____19_____. Basil looked a little uncomfortable as the _____20_____ passed and the phone remained unanswered. _____21_____ the quiz master sighed with relief as _____22_____, somewhere picked up a receiver. A well-known _____23_____ answered.

"Hello, Basil, this is the Prime Minister _____24_____."

For once in his career Basil Hall was at a loss for words. His mouth gaped open and the audience burst into laughter.

Points of View

1 List five television programmes you like, and five programmes you do not like.
 For each one in the first list give at least two reasons for liking it. For each one in the second list say what you do not like about it, and then suggest ways in which you think the programme could be improved.
2 Look through today's television programme guide. Choose two programmes you would like to watch. If possible record them on video tape so that you can see them again. Then write a review of the programmes as if for a newspaper review column:
— describe briefly what each programme is about
— say what you liked about it
— comment on anything you did not like about it
— suggest ways in which it could have been improved
Exchange your reviews with others in your group and discuss any differences of opinion.
3 Write a letter to a television station about:
a) a programme you have enjoyed,
b) a programme you did not like.

Watching TV

What do you watch on television? Have you ever wondered what other people watch and how long they spend in front of their TV sets? Do you think watching television affects us in any way?

Why not conduct a survey to find the answers to these questions? Begin by keeping a daily diary of the TV programmes you watch. Use your diary to help you think about how you watch television.

To think and talk about

What do you watch?

1 Do you plan what you watch in advance, or do you switch on and search the channels looking for an interesting programme?
2 Is there a channel you watch more than others? Can you say why this is?
3 Which programmes do you watch? Are these the same programmes your friends watch? Why do you think this is?
4 Which types of programme do you enjoy the most? Which do you hardly ever watch?
5 Do you watch video tapes? If so, do you "time shift" — watch programmes recorded at an earlier time? Do you watch hired video tapes? Are there any recorded programmes or films you enjoy watching again and again? Can you explain why this is? Do you prefer watching videos to off-air broadcasts? Why?
6 How much television do you watch in a day?

How do you watch?

1 Do you watch TV with the rest of the family?
2 Do you watch programmes in silence, or do you talk about them as you watch?
3 Do you do other things while you watch? If so, are there some programmes to which you give your full attention? Which ones are they?
4 If a programme is uninteresting do you look for another one to watch, or do you switch off the TV?
5 Do advertisements spoil your concentration?

After the programmes

1 Do you discuss what you have watched with your parents? With other adults? With your friends?
2 How much do you remember of what you see? Can you remember what happened in the programmes you watched last night? Which of them do you remember best?
    Can you remember programmes you watched last week or last year?
    Why do you think some programmes, or parts of programmes, are easier to remember?
3 Does watching a drama or film make you want to read the book it came from?
    Do you think you would read more, or less, if you did not watch television?

Read this article from the *Early Times* newspaper.

1 Do you agree with any of Juliet's views? Which of her opinions do you disagree with?
2 Make a list of the interesting things you would have time for if you watched less television.
3 Write an article pointing out the advantages of watching television.

"Did you see **Neighbours** last night?"
"Yeah, good wasn't it?"
This is the sort of conversation I hear from my friends at school.
I have never had a telly at home. I don't even know what **Neighbours** is like.
(But, I must say, I know the theme music as my friends are always singing it.)
But really, I don't think I miss much.
Whenever there is a film on like **Sparkling Cyanide**, by Agatha Christie, I just get the book of it and read that.
I don't miss out on any music because I got my own radio at Christmas.
And, when it comes to news, all I have to do is go to buy a copy of the Early Times!
I think our family is a lot closer than we would be if we had a telly.
In the evening we play games, read or do homework. We all have lots of hobbies.
So, although you telly addicts out there won't believe me, you can survive without a telly!

Juliet Buckley, 12 from North Wales

A Television Survey

Design a questionnaire to find out the viewing habits and opinions of other people. Use the ideas on these pages to help you.

Presenting your Findings

It is most important to present the results of your survey properly. Here are some suggestions.

* A pie chart is useful to show how much time people spend watching television, or the amount of time they spend watching different channels during a week.
* A top ten chart shows clearly the most popular programmes.
* Block graphs are a simple and effective way of comparing information such as the most popular TV channels.

A pie chart showing how Angela spends her leisure time. Each division represents one hour.

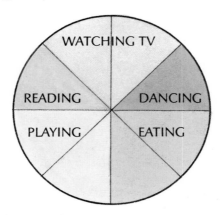

A graph showing the most popular TV channels.

WE'D BETTER SWITCH OFF. IT'S FRIGHTENING MUM AND DAD.

What other ways of presenting your information can you think of?

Is TV Real?

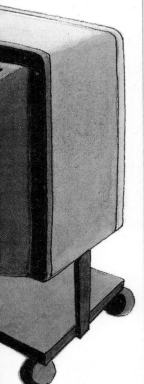

A commercial came on the screen. A little girl was swinging, and a solemn voice announced that the little girl had skinned her knee yesterday, and was about to fall on the same knee today.

Lennie looked at the girl's knee. There was a mark the size of a dime. He glanced down at his own huge, discoloured leg. He thought that the people who made television commercials didn't know anything about real life, not the way he, Lennie, did.

It seemed to him suddenly that every TV person he had ever seen wasn't real, not the girl in danger of skinning her knee again, not the women who had just given up their soap for an experiment in white clothes, not the man who had eaten enchiladas and gotten an acid stomach.

Lennie went on, even including his favourites. Not Hoss who had just won a Chinese girl in a poker game. Not Lassie who had rescued a colt from a burning barn. Not Gentle Ben who didn't really kill the chickens. Not the Brady Bunch who had to go on a talent show and sing a rock song to get money for their parents' anniversary gift.

That wasn't life. It was close enough to fool you, Lennie thought, if you weren't careful, and yet those TV characters were as different as a wax figure is from a real person. Lennie imagined you had to come up against life hard to know what it was all about.

He looked at the TV. He smiled slightly. On the screen Hoss was saying, "But, dagburnit, Pa, how was *I* to know Ming Lee was a girl?"

Lennie watched Pa for a moment. Pa Cartwright was the kind of father that would make you think — if you had a father — that your father wasn't good enough. Or Lassie pulling a new-born colt from the burning barn made you think your dog wasn't good enough. Or Mother Nature-type forests ruined real forests for you, made them seem dirty and empty. Or the Waltons or the Brady Bunch made you think there was something wrong with your family, when really, Lennie thought, his own family — just him and his mom — was a hundred times realler than the Bradys or the Waltons or the Cleavers or any other TV family you could name.

(From *The TV Kid* by Betsy Byars)

1   Why does Lennie think that people who make TV commercials know nothing about real life? Do you agree with him? What makes you think so?
2   What has Lennie suddenly realised about TV?
3   What did Lennie see as the danger of believing in characters on television? Do you think he is right?
4   Make a list of TV characters whom you think are not true to life. Can you say why you think so? Do the same with TV adverts.
5   Choose a character and an advert from your lists and say how each could be made more believable.
Would this make them more, or less, effective? Say why you think so.

Something to do
How much advertising is there on TV? You could find out by making careful notes during an hour's viewing.
1   Count the number of advertising breaks, the number of advertisements per break and the total time of each break.
What kind of audience do you think the adverts are aimed at?
2   Do the same for an hour at a different time of day. Are the adverts of the same type? Are they aimed at the same audience? Why do you think this is?

Come and Buy!

Advertisers put a great deal of time and thought into planning their advertisements so that they appeal to the right audience. They also aim their adverts at a particular feeling or emotion.

Look at these two toothpaste advertisements.

Brush regularly with **Gleam** for that sweet, confident smile. **Gleam** is the only toothpaste with *Oraltone B* for sweeter breath. Now with added fluoride for healthier teeth.

The unique three-way action of **Strongadent X** fights decay and builds healthier teeth.
1 **Strongadent X** removes plaque and unsightly tartar.
2 Its anti-bacterial action kills off the germs which cause tooth decay.
3 Its added fluoride builds stronger, healthier teeth.
Laboratory tests prove the effectiveness of **Strongadent X**. See how a single brushing with **Strongadent X** removes plaque and tartar.
Strongadent X. Dentists prefer it.

To think and talk about

A Answer these questions for each advertisement.

1 Who is the advertisement aimed at?
2 What does it offer its buyers?
3 What problems does it claim to solve for them?
4 What emotion is the advertiser aiming at?
5 How does he set out to achieve this?
6 Does he succeed?

B

1 What is the purpose of the diagrams in the **Strongadent X** advert? Do they really prove anything?
2 What are plaque and tartar?
3 What does the slogan "Dentists prefer it" really mean?
4 Do the advertisements have anything in common?
5 Which of the two toothpastes would you choose? Give reasons for your answer.

To think and talk about

1 Are you or your family influenced by TV advertisements or advertising?
2 Do you think advertising is a good or a bad thing? Give reasons for your answer.

Things to do

Design your own advertisement for one of these products:

a shampoo	a new fruit drink
a savoury snack	a new dessert

Think about whom your advertisement is to appeal to, and what emotion you are aiming at.
Try to think of a catchy slogan for your advert.

Advertising on Television

Television advertisements take much longer to develop and produce than adverts in newspapers and magazines, but they reach a wider audience and are usually much more effective. A study of them can be fascinating and rewarding.

A Looking at a TV Advert

1 Record three or four advertisements on video cassette. Choose one of them to examine in detail. Ask your teacher for activity sheet **5.3p** to help you make notes on it.
2 Try to see how many separate camera shots make up the advert. The answer will probably surprise you!
3 The advert will have been carefully planned using a story board like this one.

Watch your chosen advert again carefully. Prepare a story board for it. Use activity sheet **5.3q** to help you.

B Camera Shots

You will have noticed that an advertisement uses a number of different camera shots and that these are composed in a number of different ways. Try to match these descriptions to the pictures.

a) LS   Long shot (shows the whole person, including feet)
b) MLS   Medium long shot (down to the knees)
c) MS   Mid-shot (down to the hips)
d) MCU   Medium close-up (head and shoulders)
e) CU   Close-up (head only)
f) BCU   Big close-up (features only)

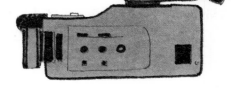

Try to identify these camera shots in your advert.
Look too for high or low camera angles and unusual viewpoints.
What effect do the different camera shots and angles have? Why do you think they were used?

Your Own TV Advert

It is quite easy to design your own TV advert. You don't even need a camera, a video or a TV set!

Designing an advert involves careful planning and the preparation of a story board. The advert may then be made into a video, but if such equipment is not available then the advert may be made into a book with a page for each separate camera shot. The pictures might be still photographs or art work.

1 Pre-planning
a) Think of a product. If you prefer you could choose one of those on page 53.
b) Think about your audience. Who will buy your product? What sort of advertisement will catch their attention? What emotion (feeling) will you be aiming at?
c) What message do you want to get across to your audience? Has your product a unique selling point, i.e. does it have something that similar products lack?

2 Planning
When you have made your pre-planning decisions it is time to think of the content of your advert.

a) Think about such things as characters, setting, the script, music and jingles, background sounds, camera shots and lighting.
b) Prepare a story board showing what will be seen and heard for each camera shot. Use sheet **5.3q** to help you.
c) Write a jingle for your advert, and record it on audio cassette.

3 Recording Your Advert

If you have video equipment you can use your prepared script and story board to record your advert. A still camera is a substitute for a video camera, but movement will of course be lost, and the advert will then be best represented in the pages of a book.

In either case use the camera viewfinder to check the effect of your story board camera angles. Don't be afraid to make changes whenever you are unhappy with your original ideas. Remember: your aim is to produce the most effective television commercial you can!

4 Evaluation
Try out your completed advertisement on your targeted audience. Did it interest them? Did they appreciate the message you were trying to get across? How much of the advert can they remember? Can they remember your slogan or jingle?

What improvements would make your advert even more effective?

Media Project
Producing your own new snack bar

KitKat is one of the most popular chocolate biscuit snacks ever produced. In 1986 over £140,000,000 worth of KitKats were sold.

If you were to create and market a *new* snack bar how would you go about it? Look at the ideas on these two pages and then have a go!

1   Market Research

There are many types of snack bar available today. If you want yours to be popular you will need to do some market research to find out what your customers want.

Perhaps your group could design a questionnaire like this one, and find out what your friends think about snack bars?

Questionnaire
Name: Sayeb Ali   *Age:* 11
Male/~~Female~~
What is your favourite snack bar?   Swoop
Why do you prefer this one?   I like the combination of flavours.
How much does the bar cost?   22p.
Do you think it is a fair price?   It is not bad value.

To think and talk about

Why do you think the questionnaire asks for the customer's age?
What other questions would your group include in your questionnaire?

2   Designing Your Biscuit

Once you have collected your information you can begin to design your snack bar. Consider what people like about their favourite snack bars. What sort of ingredients and flavours are most popular? Draw sketches of what you think your snack bar should be like.

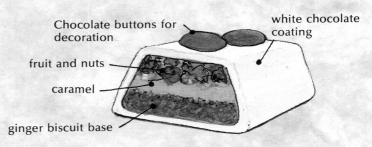

Chocolate buttons for decoration

white chocolate coating

fruit and nuts

caramel

ginger biscuit base

3   Making and Tasting

Now for the fun part! Try making your own biscuit/snack, using the recipes on activity sheets **5.3r** and **5.3s** to help you. You will need to make three or four different variations of your biscuit, because it is quite possible that people will prefer something different from what you have in mind. Don't forget to keep a careful note of the recipes you use. You will want to repeat any successful ones!

When your various samples are ready, ask people to taste test them. Design a questionnaire to record their responses. You will need to ask at least three people about your snacks, so make sure you have enough samples. In general the more tasters you have, the more reliable your results will be. Ask for comments on the appearance, taste and texture of your snack samples.

Questionnaire

Sample 1	Sample 2	Sample 3	Sample 4
Pleasant but much too sweet.	I like the caramel but it is a little too sticky.	Much too soggy.	This tastes just like a Mammoth Bar!

To think and talk about

Read through your tasters' responses. Is your snack bar good enough? What did they like about it? What needs to be improved? Make any necessary changes to your recipe and re-test your improved versions. There are bound to be lots of volunteers for the tastings!

4 Marketing Your Snack Bar

Now you have settled on a recipe for your snack bar, you will need to think of a name for it. Discuss possibilities with your group. Make a list of the names you like best, and ask other people which one they think sounds the most exciting.

When you have decided on a name for your snack/biscuit, try designing an interesting and eye-catching logo for it.

Your next task will be to work out a selling price. This will largely depend on the cost of the ingredients you have used and the size of your snack bar. You should also consider other factors such as: — the cost of making the snack (gas/electricity)
— the cost of wrappings
— advertising material (paper and materials for posters, etc.)
— how much (if any) profit you wish to make

To think and talk about

When you have reached a price, compare it with the price of other snacks on the market. If yours is more expensive will anyone want to buy it?
It might be worth considering special introductory offers to create interest in your product.

5 Packaging

This is a very important part of the product, and it should look as attractive as possible. Look carefully at the packaging of other snacks on the market. What else do they feature besides the logo and the price? Look at the reverse of this KitKat wrapper.

Perhaps you could incorporate some of these ideas into your wrapper? Suggestions on designing and making different types of packaging are given on activity sheet 5.3t.

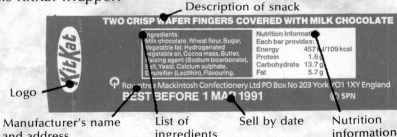

6 Advertising

Making people aware that your product exists is vital. The makers of KitKat try to ensure their product is kept in the public's mind by careful advertising and consumer promotions. As well as giant posters which can be seen from cars, buses and trains, Rowntree also make use of television commercials.

For you to do

a) KitKat has a catchy jingle, with the slogan: "Have a break — have a KitKat!"
   Think of a catchy jingle for your own product.
b) Design an eye-catching poster suitable for a roadside hoarding.
c) Write a T.V. advertisement for your snack. Use Level 5 Cassette to help you (side 2, track 1).

UNIT 4   The Titanic

The White Star liner *Titanic*, the largest and most luxurious vessel in the world set out from Southampton on 10th April, 1912 bound for New York on her maiden voyage. Some claimed she was unsinkable, yet four days later she struck an iceberg in the North Atlantic and sank with the loss of 1500 lives. In this unit we look at the events of that tragic night. It is a story that has fascinated people for the best part of a century.

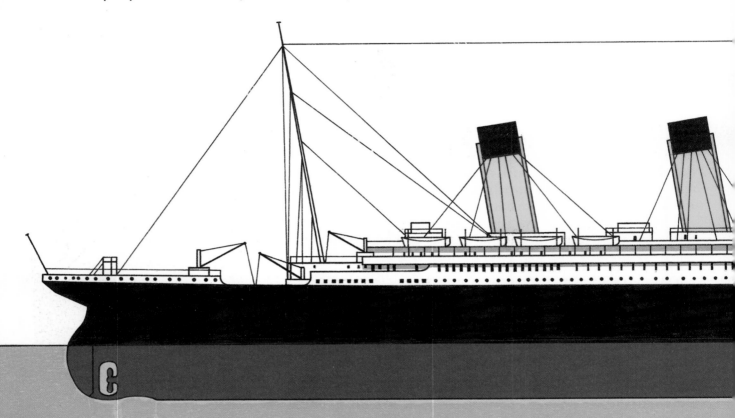

Captain Smith

1   The *Titanic* was a magnificent ship. She was 270m long and weighed 46,388 tonnes. She had a double bottom and sixteen water-tight compartments which could be sealed in an emergency. Some people believed this made her unsinkable. Her cabins and state rooms were the most luxurious on any liner. She had shops, a gymnasium, squash court, swimming pool, Turkish bath, restaurant and a cafe. Her 2,200 passengers, among them some of the richest people of the time, felt they were on the safest and most luxurious vessel ever built.

2   During the voyage the *Titanic* received various ice warnings, but ice was not unusual in April in the North Atlantic. At 1.42 p.m. on Sunday, April 14th a warning of icebergs 250 miles ahead of the *Titanic* was received and given to Captain Smith, but a later warning was not sent to the bridge.

3   At 5.50 p.m. Captain Smith altered the ship's course slightly to the south. At 7.30 p.m. three warning messages about large icebergs were received from the *Californian*. These were delivered to the bridge, but the Captain was attending a dinner party below. The ice was now only fifty miles ahead. At 8.55 p.m. Captain Smith came on the bridge and discussed the situation with Second Officer Lightoller, and at 9.20 p.m. he retired for the night with orders to wake him "if it becomes at all doubtful . . ." In those days it was normal for ships to travel at full speed until an iceberg was actually sighted. That night was clear, and the sea unusually calm. At 9.30 p.m. Lightoller sent a message to the lookouts in the crow's nest to watch carefully for icebergs.

4   In the wireless room of the *Titanic*, the operator cut off another ice warning from the *Californian* just 19 miles to the north, because he was trying to send messages to the wireless station in Newfoundland which was now just in range.

5   At 11.40 p.m. one of the lookouts in the crow's nest, Frederick Fleet, saw something directly ahead, growing larger. "Iceberg right ahead," he reported to the bridge. Lightoller had now been relieved by Sixth Officer James Moody, who ordered the engines stopped and reversed. He called for the ship to be turned to port and pulled a lever to close the watertight compartments in the bottom of the ship. The *Titanic* took a few moments to respond and then began to turn slowly to port. It was too late. It hit the iceberg a glancing blow along its starboard bow, tearing an estimated 80 metre gash in the side of the ship below the water-line. The ship shuddered slightly and then came slowly to a stop.

6   Most of the passengers were unaware of what had happened. One or two rushed on deck in time to see the iceberg disappearing behind them. Some ice had fallen into the well deck and jokes were made about putting some in the drinks or playing football with it in the morning. Other passengers continued to play cards, or decided to turn in for the night.

7   In the boiler room at the bottom of the ship there was a sound like "the roar of thunder" as icy water poured in. Within twenty minutes water was flooding the first five of the watertight compartments in the bottom of the ship. Captain Smith knew the *Titanic* was doomed.

Frederick Fleet

Titanic 11.58 April 14th — Distress Call Sig. Loud

CQD – SOS We have from ~~CQD~~ M.G.Y fast come to our assistance Position Lat 41.46 n. Lon. 50 14 w We have struck iceberg sinking MGY

8 At 12.05 a.m. Captain Smith went to the wireless room and gave instructions to send out the standard distress signal, CQD. The SOS signal was just coming into use and the operator decided to send this too. It was the first time the new signal had ever been used at sea. When a ship was seen about ten miles to the north, Captain Smith ordered white distress rockets to be sent up. At 12.25 a.m. he ordered the lifeboats to be loaded with women and children. He knew that although the *Titanic* carried more lifeboats than the British Board of Trade requirements, there were enough for only half the passengers.

9 On the nearby *Californian* the radio operator had gone off duty at 11.30 p.m. as was the practice at the time, so the CDQ and SOS calls were not heard. After midnight officers on the bridge of the *Californian* saw white rockets bursting over an unidentified liner to the south. They suspected that the ship was in trouble and reported to Captain Lord who was below deck. He asked what colour the rockets were, and then ordered the liner to be signalled with a Morse lamp, but she disappeared without replying.

10 Most of the passengers continued to be unaware of the seriousness of the situation, until the deck began to tilt and the distress rockets were fired. Even when Second Officer Lightoller began to load the lifeboats with women and children, many people chose to stay on the apparently safe ship, where the band continued to play lively music. When the first lifeboat was lowered into the water it held only 28 people, although it had room for 65. One, with a capacity of forty, held only twelve. Lightoller had been ordered to turn men away until all the women and children were loaded, but many women refused to leave their husbands and stayed on board. The ever-increasing tilt of the Titanic caused the final boat to be swept overboard without being loaded. When all the boats had gone a calm fell on the remaining passengers. Captain Smith went round the ship telling everyone, "Now it's every man for himself."

Lifeboats being loaded

Funnel for auxiliary Machinery & Ventilation

SPACE OCCUPIED BY RECIPROCATING & TURBINE ENGINES

WATER LINE

Two Forward Funnels carrying off Products of Combustion from Main Boilers

SPACE OCCUPIED BY BOILERS

11   At 2.18 a.m. a huge roar was heard as the ship broke in two and the ship's boilers crashed downwards. The lights, which had burned throughout the crisis, finally went out. As the bow section sank, the stern righted itself for a short time before it too slid down beneath the icy waters. It was 2.20 a.m. and over 1500 passengers had been lost.

12   The *Carpathia* was the nearest ship to the Titanic at the time. She came into the area at 3.30 a.m. Over the next five hours she took on board all 705 survivors from the lifeboats. As the *Californian* arrived to continue the search, the *Carpathia* set off for New York.

About the Disaster

Read carefully the account of the *Titanic's* voyage, and then answer these questions.

A

1 In what ways was the *Titanic* the most luxurious vessel in the world?
2 Why was she considered unsinkable?
3 What actions did Captain Smith take as a result of the iceberg warnings?
4 Why did he allow the *Titanic* to proceed at full speed?
5 Why did the wireless operator cut off the last ice warning from the *Californian*?
6 At what point did Captain Smith know that the *Titanic* was doomed?

B

1 Look at the distress message sent out by the wireless operators. What evidence is there that both distress signals were used?
2 Explain why the passengers were unaware of the seriousness of the situation.
3 What made them aware of real danger?
4 Why were there lifeboats for only half the passengers?
5 Explain why many passengers chose not to go in the lifeboats.
6 Why do you think Lightoller **a)** refused to allow men on the lifeboats? **b)** allowed the lifeboats to be lowered when they were not full?
7 What would you have done in Lightoller's situation? Give reasons for your answers.
8 Why do you think Captain Lord of the *Californian* took so little action? What would you have done in his place? Give reasons for your answer.

C   The Main Idea

1 Write the numbers of the paragraphs which tell us about the ice warnings and the precautions taken as a result.
2 Which paragraphs describe the effects of the collision with the iceberg?
3 Paragraph 8 deals with the actions taken by Captain Smith to save his passengers and crew. What is the main idea of each of the last four paragraphs?

D

1 Describe what each of the following did after Frederick Fleet had sighted the iceberg:
   a) James Moody   **b)** Captain Smith   **c)** Second Officer Lightoller.
2 Ask your teacher for activity sheet **5.4a.** Complete the timeline showing what happened on the night of the 14th/15th April, 1912.
3 Make a list of all the factors which contributed to the disaster.

The Inquiries

There were two inquiries into the disaster, one in the U.S.A., because the *Titanic* was American owned, and the other by the British Board of Trade.

The United States Senate Inquiry took place first. They were particularly concerned that a far higher proportion of the richer passengers were saved than those from the third class, but the White Star Line denied giving any preference. During the British Inquiry the full figures were made known.

	First Class			Second Class			Third Class			Crew
	Men	Women	Children	Men	Women	Children	Men	Women	Children	
Saved	58	139	5	13	78	24	55	98	23	210
Lost	115	5	0	147	15	0	399	81	53	688

It should be remembered that the third class passengers had cabins on the lower decks. Those who made their way up the staircases found their way to the Boat Deck blocked by barriers dividing the third class from the first, but some managed to find a way round or broke them down.

The U.S. Inquiry also criticised the lifeboat loading: so few of them were full, and only one boat turned back to pick up more survivors.

Both inquiries condemned Captain Lord of the *Californian* for his inaction when the distress rockets were seen. He maintained that the strange ship to the south was not the *Titanic*, but some other ship, and that when she disappeared she was still afloat. Neither committee believed his story. In his defence it is worth noting that in 1912 there was no standard procedure for distress signals, and that some shipping companies used white rockets to make private signals to sister ships.

The British Inquiry concluded that the *Titanic* had been lost because of her excessive speed at the time of the collision.

To think and talk about

1   Look at the Board of Trade figures above. What do they show about the proportion of first class passengers saved to those in third class? Can you explain why this was?
    How successfully do you think Captain Smith's order to save the women and children was carried out?

2   One of the results of the inquiry was the shifting of summer shipping routes ninety five kilometres further south, reducing the danger of icebergs.
    Read again the account of the disaster and the findings of the inquiries. Make a list of all the changes you can think of which would make subsequent sea crossings safer.

3   Stage your own inquiry into the *Titanic* disaster. The book *A Night to Remember* by Walter Lord gives a detailed account of the sinking, but if you cannot find a copy then refer to the material in this unit.
    Two children might take the roles of Second Officer Lightoller, and Frederick Fleet, the lookout. Other children take the parts of survivors from first, second and third class, the captains of the *Californian* and *Carpathia*, and Second Officer Stone and Apprentice Officer Gibson from the *Californian* who believed the ship they saw to the south was beginning to list. The rest of the group then make up the inquiry committee. They must ask questions, consider the answers, arrive at conclusions and make recommendations for improved safety at sea.

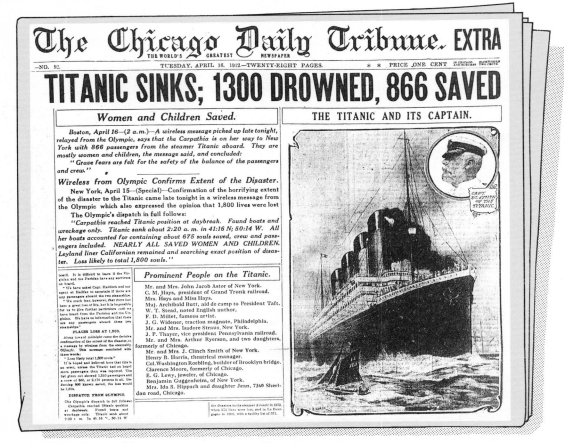

The Chicago Daily Tribune. EXTRA

THE WORLD'S GREATEST NEWSPAPER

—NO. 92.　　　TUESDAY, APRIL 16, 1912—TWENTY-EIGHT PAGES.　　　* * PRICE ONE CENT　IN CHICAGO AND SUBURBS ELSEWHERE TWO CENTS

TITANIC SINKS; 1300 DROWNED, 866 SAVED

Women and Children Saved.

Boston, April 16—(2 a.m.)—A wireless message picked up late tonight, relayed from the Olympic, says that the Carpathia is on her way to New York with 866 passengers from the steamer Titanic aboard. They are mostly women and children, the message said, and concluded:

"Grave fears are felt for the safety of the balance of the passengers and crew."

Wireless from Olympic Confirms Extent of the Disaster.

New York, April 15—(Special)—Confirmation of the horrifying extent of the disaster to the Titanic came late tonight in a wireless message from the Olympic which also expressed the opinion that 1,800 lives were lost

The Olympic's dispatch in full follows:

"Carpathia reached Titanic position at daybreak. Found boats and wreckage only. Titanic sank about 2:20 a.m. in 41:16 N; 50:14 W. All her boats accounted for containing about 675 souls saved, crew and passengers included. NEARLY ALL SAVED WOMEN AND CHILDREN. Leyland liner Californian remained and searching exact position of disaster. Loss likely to total 1,800 souls."

Prominent People on the Titanic.

Mr. and Mrs. John Jacob Astor of New York.
C. M. Hays, president of Grand Trunk railroad.
Mrs. Hays and Miss Hays.
Maj. Archibald Butt, aid de camp to President Taft.
W. T. Stead, noted English author.
F. D. Millet, famous artist.
J. G. Widener, traction magnate, Philadelphia.
Mr. and Mrs. Isadore Straus, New York.
J. P. Thayer, vice president Pennsylvania railroad.
Mr. and Mrs. Arthur Ryerson, and two daughters, formerly of Chicago.
Mr. and Mrs. J. Clinch Smith of New York.
Henry B. Harris, theatrical manager.
Col. Washington Roebling, builder of Brooklyn bridge.
Clarence Moore, formerly of Chicago.
E. G. Lewy, jeweler, of Chicago.
Benjamin Guggenheim, of New York.
Mrs. Ida S. Hippach and daughter Jean, 7360 Sheridan road, Chicago.

THE TITANIC AND ITS CAPTAIN.

CAPT. E.C. SMITH OF THE TITANIC.

A Both these newspapers appeared on April 16th, 1912, but look at the very different stories they tell! Can you think of any reason for this?

1 How accurate is *The Chicago Tribune's* report?

2 How accurate is the report in *The Daily Mirror*?

3 Look at the dates and times of the messages reported in both papers. Which has the more up to date information? Can you think of a reason for this?

B Scan *The Daily Mirror* for the answers to these questions.

1 The paper states that "the one all-important and outstanding fact (is) that — Every man, woman and child on the great liner is safe."
Write down the message which claims this to be true.

2 Write down two messages about the passengers which are contradictory.

3 Write down two messages about the recovery of the *Titanic* which are contradictory.

4 Write down the message you think is closest to what really happened.

5 Can you think of any reason why these messages are so very wrong?

6 Do you think the headlines and leading paragraphs are a fair summary of the messages received? Give reasons for your answer.

7 To what does the paper say the passengers owe their lives? Do you agree with this?

8 Why do you think the messages from the *Titanic* were "blurred"?

C **Writing**

1 Write the headlines and opening paragraphs you think would have appeared in *The Daily Mirror* had they had more accurate and up to date information.

2 Imagine you are one of the survivors of the disaster. Write the full story from the moment you got on board the *Titanic* to your rescue by the *Carpathia*. Describe the magnificence of the *Titanic*, the collision with the iceberg, how you gradually became aware that the liner was sinking and your evacuation in a lifeboat on the icy waters. Describe what you saw, heard and felt as the liner broke up and sank.

EVERY ONE ON BOARD WORLD'S GREATEST LINER SAFE AFTER COLLISION WITH ICE

TITANIC'S WIRELESS SIGNAL BRINGS VESSELS TO SCENE.

46,000-Ton Ship, with 2,300 Aboard, in Peril.

EVERYONE SAFE.

Morning of Suspense Ends in Message of Relief.

PASSENGERS TAKEN OFF.

Helpless Giant Being Towed to Port by Allan Liner.

The White Star liner Titanic, the greatest ship the world has ever known, has met with disaster on her maiden voyage.

She left Southampton on Wednesday last and carried about 2,300 passengers and crew on board, with 3,400 sacks of mails.

On Sunday she came into collision with an iceberg, and immediately flashed out wireless messages for help.

Many steamers rushed to her aid, but her fate and that of the thousands on board remained in doubt on both sides of the Atlantic for many hours.

It was at length known that every soul was safe, and that the vessel itself was proceeding to Halifax (Nova Scotia), towed by the Allan liner Virginian.

All her passengers had by that time been taken aboard two of the liners that hurried to the scene in reply to the wireless message.

DRAMATIC TELEGRAMS OF DISASTER

So many and so conflicting were the reports that reached London yesterday concerning the fate of the Titanic that until detailed and definite tidings come to hand it is difficult to establish much more than the one all-important and outstanding fact that—

Every man, woman and child on the great liner is safe.

It would appear that once again the value to humanity of wireless telegraphy has been established, for at least five vessels are known to have hastened to the aid of the world's greatest ship when she flashed forth her appeal for help.

Three at least arrived in time to be of the greatest service, as is evident from the following series of dramatic Reuter messages which reached London yesterday at the times named (N.B.—New York time is five hours behind London):—

6.15 a.m. (New York).—A telegram received here from Montreal says:—

"The liner Virginian reports in a wireless communication that the liner Titanic, which is reported to have been in collision with an iceberg, has requested assistance. The Virginian is hastening to her aid."

8.40 a.m. (New York).—A telegram from Cape Race says:—

"The wireless telegraph operator on board the Titanic reported the weather calm and clear, the position of the liner being then 41.46 north, 50.14 west.

"The Virginian at midnight was 170 miles west of the Titanic, and is expected to reach her at ten o'clock this morning.

"The Olympic at midnight was in 40.32 north latitude, 61.18 west longitude. She is also in direct communication with the Titanic, and is hastening to her."

BLURRED MESSAGES.

8.45 a.m. (New York).—The liner Baltic has also reported herself within 200 miles of the Titanic, and says she is speeding to her help.

The last signals from the Titanic came at 12.27 this morning. The Virginian's operator says that these were blurred and ended abruptly.—Reuter.

9.5 a.m. (New York).—A telegram from Cape Race says: "At 10.25 on Sunday evening the Titanic reported she had struck an iceberg. The steamer said that immediate assistance was required.

"Half an hour afterwards another message was received saying that the Titanic was sinking by the head, and that the women were being taken off in lifeboats."—Reuter.

1.50 p.m. (New York).—Up to this hour the officials of the White Star Line have not received a word regarding the reported accident to the Titanic. The company have issued the following statement:—

"Twelve hours have passed since the collision of the Titanic is reported to have taken place. We have heard nothing of an accident.

"It is very strange that the Titanic's sister ship Olympic, which has a wireless installation of sufficient strength to send a message across the Atlantic, should have sent us nothing. The Olympic should be alongside the Titanic at two this afternoon."

2.50 p.m. (New York).—A dispatch from Halifax states that all the passengers of the Titanic had left the ship by 3.30 this morning.

3.5 p.m. (New York).—The Montreal Star reports from Halifax that the Titanic is still afloat and is making her way slowly to Halifax.

4.50 p.m. (New York).—A message from Montreal timed 8.30 a.m. says:—

"The Titanic is still afloat and heading towards Halifax with her own engines.

"The women and children have not been taken off, though the lifeboats are ready in case of emergency. It is thought that the bulkheads will prevent her sinking."

A later message says: "Wireless telegraphy brings the word that two vessels are standing by the Titanic, and that all the passengers have been taken off."

5.20 p.m. (New York).—"The transfer of the passengers from the Titanic is now being carried out. Twenty boat loads have already been taken on board the Cunarder Carpathia."

This last report was sent by wireless telegraphy to Mr. Franklin, vice-president of the White Star Company in New York, by Captain Haddock, of the Olympic, which is nearing the Titanic.

The dispatch adds that the Parisian and Carpathia are in attendance on the Titanic, and that the Baltic is nearing the ship.

Unofficial telegrams state that the Virginian has taken the Titanic in tow.

7.40 p.m. (New York).—Mr. Franklin at one o'clock this afternoon gave out the following message received from the Boston office of the White Star Line:—

"Allan line, Montreal, confirms report Virginian, Parisian and Carpathia in attendance, standing by Titanic."

PASSENGERS TRANSHIPPED.

MONTREAL, April 15.—It is now confirmed here that the passengers of the Titanic have been safely transhipped to the Allan liner Parisian and the Cunarder Carpathia.

The Virginian is still towing the Titanic towards Halifax.—Exchange.

NO LIVES IN DANGER.

NEW YORK, April 15.—The White Star officials here state that the Virginian is standing by the Titanic and that there is no danger of loss of life.

A wireless telegraph message to Halifax states that all the passengers were safely taken off the Titanic at 3.30.

Mr. Franklin, vice-president of the White Star Company, states that the Titanic is unsinkable. The fact that she was reported to have sunk several feet by the head was, he said, unimportant. She could go down many feet at the head as the result of water filling the forward compartments and yet remain afloat indefinitely.—Exchange.

STRUGGLING TOWARDS PORT.

NEW YORK, April 15.—A wireless message received at Boston from St. John's, Newfoundland, states that the Titanic is slowly struggling towards Cape Race.

An unsigned wireless message, timed 8.30, has been received at Montreal, stating that the Titanic

MR. BRIDE.   **MR. CRAIG.**

Mr. Norman C. Craig, K.C., is a passenger on the Titanic. Mr. Harold Bride is the junior wireless operator on board.—(Elliott and Fry and Runciman.)

is still afloat, and is slowly steaming towards Halifax, Nova Scotia.

The forward compartments are full of water, but if the vessel is able to withstand the strain it is hoped to make port.

News has now reached here that at 11.10 a.m. (Canadian time) the local agents of the White Star Line at Montreal received another wireless message confirming the earlier reports that the Titanic was not only afloat but that the liner's engines were also working.

At this time the local agents were not aware whether the Virginian was with the Titanic, but they believed that she was standing by, and that possibly the women and children might have already been transferred.—Exchange Telegraph

LLOYD'S MESSAGE.

According to a Lloyd's telegram, the signal station at Cape Race cabled yesterday as follows:—

"10.25 p.m. yesterday (Sunday) the Titanic reports by wireless that she has struck an iceberg, and calls for immediate assistance. At 11 p.m. she was reported sinking by head. Women being put off in boats. Gave her position as 41.46 N., 50.14 W.

"Steamers Baltic, Olympic, and Virginian are all making towards the scene of the disaster. The latter was the last to hear the Titanic's signals. At 12.27 a.m. to-day (Monday) she reported them, then blurred and ending abruptly. It is believed that the Virginian will be the first ship to reach the Titanic."

WONDER OF WIRELESS.

Thanks to the wonderful modern invention of wireless telegraphy, which ten years ago was unknown, the Titanic was able to flash messages over the ocean asking for aid.

The wireless signal for "assistance wanted" is now "S.O.S.," the more familiar letters, "C.Q.D.," having been abandoned because they led to confusion with other code signals.

As a result of these "S.O.S." messages, five ships went to the assistance of the Titanic—the Baltic and the Olympic, of the White-Star Line; the Virginian and the Parisian, of the Allan Line, and the Cunarder Carpathia. The two last named took off boat-loads of passengers.

Thus the passengers of the Titanic owe their safety to the invention of wireless, to the wondrous discovery of which it is due that every large liner is now in communication with any liner or battleship within hundreds of miles.

On the high seas in these days one has only, as it were, to touch a button to give the alarm and immediately there is a general rush to aid. The ocean, it may almost be said, is as well guarded as London by her fire brigade.

Every wireless operator on every ship has his ear glued eternally to the receiver, waiting for messages from the vasty deep. Suddenly taps out . . . — . . . . S.O.S. It spells out HELP. He is all alert to locate the sender of the message, and then the rush across the ocean on the errand of deliverance.

A marvellous picture this of man's battle with the weapons of science against the cruel forces of elemental nature.

The Discovery of the Titanic

In the summer of 1986 Dr. Robert D. Ballard guided a tiny three-man submarine, four kilometres below the surface of the North Atlantic, and landed on the deck of the *Titanic*. Attached to the submarine was a remote-controlled robotic craft which he guided around the wreck taking photographs and video pictures. He disturbed as little as he could, treating the site as a memorial to those who had perished there.

The following year an expedition with different views removed objects from the site and brought them to the surface. Many people were horrified, especially when it was announced that a safe from the wreck would be opened on television.

Read carefully the account from Dr. Ballard's book (below), and the article opposite from the *Sunday Times* of the 3rd November, 1987. Look for answers to the questions on page 67.

As we finished our repast, the safe began to emerge at the edge of the arc illuminated by our headlights. Very gently, so as not to disturb more mud than necessary, our pilot swung us around until the object of our interest was directly outside my starboard window. It sat with its door face-up. The handle looked like it was made of gold though it had to be brass. Right next to it, I could see a small circular gold dial and above both a nice shiny gold crest. I could make out figures facing one another — they looked like horses or unicorns rearing up on their hind legs — but the crest was too small for me to read the lettering.

I directed Jim to bring *Alvin's* sample-gathering arm around for a picture. As he did so, I realized that the claw was going to practically touch the safe's handle — why not try to open it? So I watched as the arm's metal fingers locked onto the handle and its wrist began to rotate clockwise. To my surprise it turned easily, then stopped. But the door wouldn't budge, its flanges apparently rusted shut. For a moment, I felt a little like the kid caught with his hand in the cookie jar. It would be so easy to bring the safe back with us to the surface. We'd lifted heavier things with *Alvin*.

I looked at Jim and he looked back at me.

"What now?" he asked.

There was a long pause as I considered the possibilities, and imagined what the safe might contain. What would I have done if we'd opened it to discover something valuable — the bejeweled *Rubaiyat of Omar Khayyam,* for instance? I probably would have called the surface and told them to radio Woods Hole: "Have found priceless *Titanic* artifact. Please advise." Fortunately, my vow not to return with *Titanic* salvage wasn't put to the test. Probably the safe was empty, anyway. I remembered Bill Tantum telling me once that supposedly the ship's second-class safes had been opened by the crew and emptied during the final moments before the *Titanic* sank. Lawrence Beesley recalled in his account of the sinking that he had heard the door of the assistant purser's safe clang back shut after it had been emptied. Since it was apparent on closer examination that this was clearly one of the safes from the second-class purser's office, it was unlikely that it had ever held real treasure. Perhaps it contained some money and not-too-expensive jewelry. It would have been wonderful to find out.

"Let go of it and let me take some more pictures," I finally replied. If I could pass this souvenir up, I could pass up anything. (When I later examined the photos I took, I could see that the bottom of the safe had rusted out. Any contents ought to have been visible on the sediment underneath, but we saw no sign of them.)

(From *The Discovery of the Titanic* by Dr. Robert D. Ballard)

Anger at TV show's safe from Titanic

by Tony Rocca, Nice
and
Askold Krushelnycky

THE ACRIMONY and confusion still being generated by the globally-televised opening last month of what was said to be the safe found near the sunken liner Titanic are bound to strengthen the case of those who condemn the excavation as grave-robbing.

Arguments are raging about the authenticity of the items dredged up from the liner's hulk. Many millions of television viewers who expected to see the actual Titanic safe were presented with only a fragment of it inside a modern strongbox.

When the discovery of the safe was announced by the Anglo-French expedition in August, it was said to be sealed. It was to be opened only during the television broadcast, which was seen last month by an estimated world-wide audience of 100m. The dredging-up of a satchel near the wreck was also announced, and its contents of jewellery and soggy banknotes were to be revealed.

Public and press believed that the programme, hosted by the Kojak actor, Telly Savalas, would show the safe being opened and its contents revealed for the first time. What viewers finally saw were two modern safes, one containing what is left of the Titanic safe, and the other the satchel full of jewellery.

Westgate Entertainment, the television company that sold the programme rights, while not deliberately fuelling the misbeliefs, did nothing to dispel them.

Since the programme was screened, the expedition leader, together with one of his divers, Westgate Entertainments and the chief of Sygma, the picture agency that bought exclusive rights to the survey photographs, have been involved in a row over alleged "manipulation" of publicity for the show.

Last week Commander Yvon Rowarch, who co-ordinated the expedition, admitted that not only had the safe been opened hours after coming to the surface but that the safe shown on television was not from the Titanic.

He said: "The real safe was in such a pitiful state. All that held it together was its armoured door. We had to open it and replace it."

According to Jean Louis-Coppin, one of the divers, the safe was opened five hours after surfacing and contained only a leather purse with coins in it.

Westgate Entertainment sold broadcasting rights to the programme, and speculation mounted that the safe — nobody had mentioned the modern ones eventually used — contained the treasures of wealthy passengers.

Last Sunday Hubert Henrotte, the president of Sygma, said photographs showed the safe was empty when it was retrieved. He said: "Any objects of value that were to be presented during the big American show could not have come from this safe, but likely were recovered from around the wreck."

Doug Llewelyn, one of the Westgate producers admitted yesterday that "people got jumbled up about what was going to be shown". He said the original safe had almost entirely disintegrated. The safe's contents were known hours after it surfaced and only the door was displayed within the modern safe, giving the illusion of an intact strongbox. He denied there had been deliberate deception, but there had been "some set-dressing".

Critics said the site should be left as an international memorial to the 1,500 people who died when the Titanic sank in 1912. The US Congress has banned for-profit display of the objects.

1 Why did Dr. Ballard decide not to bring the safe back to the surface?
2 What did he notice when he examined the photographs later?
3 What did television viewers expect to see? What did they really see?
4 Do you think they were deliberately misled? Give reasons for your answer.
5 Who knew the truth about the safe? Why do you think they said nothing about it until later?
6 What were the facts about the safe and its contents?
7 Do you agree with the views expressed in the final paragraph of the newspaper report? Give a reason for your answer.

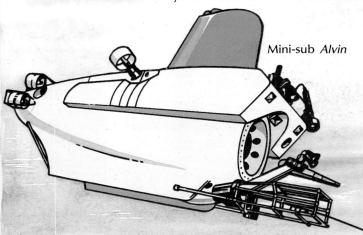

Mini-sub *Alvin*

Things to do

1 The latitude and longitude of the wreck of the *Titanic* is now known to be 49° 56′ W, 41° 43′ N. Use an atlas to find where this is. Which is the nearest land to this position?
2 Find out the difference between wireless and telegraph messages. Write a paragraph about each one.
3 Find out about the *Lusitania* and other disasters at sea.

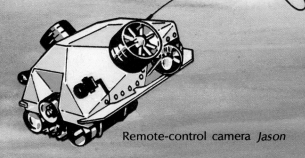

Remote-control camera *Jason*

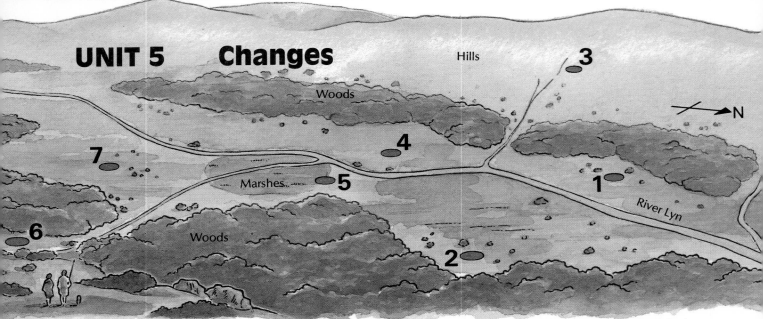

The Angles and Saxons who invaded Britain in the fifth century AD looked for places suitable for farming. Ideal sites had a supply of water, fertile soil, and a nearby timber supply. They could also be easily defended.

When Chard brought his people to the valley of the River Lyn he looked carefully for such a site. The river and its three streams offered good drinking water.

The soil on the hills was poor, but near the river it was deep and fertile.

The valley was wooded on both sides, offering wood for fuel, building materials, and for making tools, but there was also plenty of clear flat land by the river on which to grow crops and graze cattle. Chard noticed that some of this land was marshy and liable to flooding.

After some consideration Chard identified seven possible sites. Imagine you have been sent to examine each place. Write down what you would tell him about each one.

First say where each site is. Then make notes on the suitability of the site under these headings: **a)** Water **b)** Soil **c)** Wood **d)** Defence

Read through your notes carefully and select the most suitable site for Chard's farm. Give reasons for your choice.

Anglo-Saxon Place Names

Many place names in Britain are of Anglo-Saxon origin, and usually date from 500-900AD.

Anglo Saxon Names

-*ley*, -*leigh* = pasture or clearing
-*worth* = enclosure or field
-*ton* = farm or town
-*ham* = village, farm, meadow or pasture
-*wick*, -*wich* = farm

A   The site that Chard's people settled on later became known as Chadwick. Can you explain how this name came about?

B   Match these place names with their meanings.

Immingham	Bloc's enclosure	Birmingham	village of Imma's people
Bickleigh	butter farm	Hintlesham	town of Gilla's people
Gillington	Beormund's pasture	Butterwick	Bicca's pasture
Bloxworth	Hyntel's village		

Treasure Trove

When Chard's people settled, they and their descendants threw away or lost objects over the centuries. These treasures lie deep in the soil, in rubbish pits, in the ashes of long dead fires, or under the water in rivers and streams. Coins and jewels may be worth thousands of pounds, but even everyday objects from earlier times are fascinating, because they show a way of life that has gone forever.

Read this article on treasure trove carefully. If you should find anything valuable in your area it would be wise to remember the advice it gives.

'FINDERS KEEPERS' NO GOLDEN RULE

Treasure trove sites plundered at night

Gold-diggers exposed this week.

SIMON Drake, a Dorset farmer, could not believe his luck when earlier this year he walked out of Christie's saleroom more than £60,000 richer.

This was the sum that 95 medieval gold coins weighing 23 ounces realised when placed on the auction block. Mr Drake found them while preparing a field to sow a variety of barley, appropriately named Golden Promise.

The find was promptly reported to the police, which is just as well, for Mr Drake could have been charged with stealing under the Theft Act 1968 and would not have been that £60,000 better off.

In England and Wales objects of gold and silver found hidden — rather than lost or abandoned — in the ground or in buildings, are treasure trove and the property of the Crown — Providing of course the original owner cannot be found.

All finds of gold and silver should be reported to the local coroner directly or through the police or a museum. The coroner decides what is treasure trove. He holds an inquest, with a jury just as he does in cases of sudden or unnatural death. Outside Scotland, base metal objects are not treasure trove and need not be reported to the coroner. However, there may be a duty to report finds to the police or the owner of the land or building concerned. Such discoveries should also be reported to the local museum.

Matters are slightly different north of the Border. All objects, regardless of what they are made and whether they were hidden or simply lost, are treasure trove. As there are no coroners in Scotland, the police and museums report finds to the procurator fiscal.

Finders of treasure trove have no legal entitlement to keep it or to receive a reward. However when a find is declared promptly, the finder may expect to receive an ex gratia reward equivalent to the full market valuation of any treasure which is required by museums. Unwanted items will be returned for disposal or retention.

It is in the interest of finders to report their discoveries as quickly as possible. If there is concealment or undue delay the reward will be withheld or substantially reduced.

This is what happened to the finder of the Thetford treasure trove in 1979. The find, comprising Roman gold jewellery and silver items, was not declared for six months. During that period the site was built on and the opportunity of examining important archaeological evidence was lost.

As the finder was suffering from a serious illness at the time an exceptional ex-gratia payment of one third of the market value of the treasure was made — £87,180 as opposed to £261,540.

The finder of 61 Celtic gold coins at Farmborough, near Bath, failed to declare his find. Instead, he attempted to sell it through a United Kingdom dealer in the United States. The dealer became suspicious and advised the British Museum.

The coins, valued at £12,000 were declared treasure trove. The finder received no reward and the coins were confiscated.

So, if any hidden objects are found do not adopt the "Finders Keepers" attitude, but inform the authorities. Failure to do so could be expensive in more ways than one.

Andrew Moore

1 If you find gold or silver objects what should you do?
2 Explain what is considered to be treasure trove: **a)** in England and Wales, **b)** in Scotland.

3 Explain what might happen in each of these cases:
   a) a finder fails to report his find and attempts to sell it
   b) he keeps his find for a while before reporting it
   c) he reports his find immediately
4 Can a finder of hidden objects demand a reward? Give a reason for your answer.

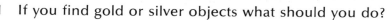

The Chadwick Bypass

Chard's farm grew over the centuries into the busy town of Chadwick.

Today the streets of Chadwick are congested with traffic passing through the town.

A solution to this problem is a bypass: a new road to carry traffic around the town.

Look at this map.

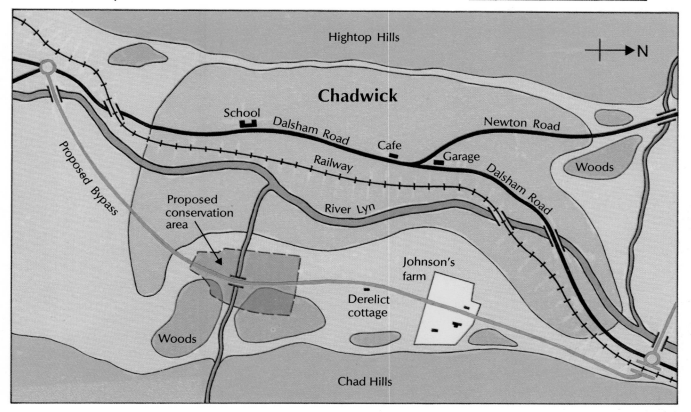

A   At the moment it takes a driver 15 minutes to travel through Chadwick on the Dalsham Road. Use the scale on the map and a piece of string to work out:

1   how long his journey is between the locations of the two proposed roundabouts (shown in red).

2   his average speed for the journey.

B   The red line shows the proposed route of the bypass.

1   Do you think the bypass is longer or shorter than the road through the town?

2   Measure the route along the proposed bypass between the two roundabouts. How long is the new route? By how much is it longer or shorter than the route through the town?

3   How long would it take to travel along the proposed bypass between the two roundabouts at a speed of 100km per hour?

4   How much time would be saved?

C

1   Write a short paragraph describing the traffic problem in Chadwick.

2   Write a second paragraph explaining how a bypass would solve the problem.

D   Besides the proposed route of the bypass the map shows a conservation area which local people had asked for. Unfortunately the bypass means this idea will have to be abandoned.

1   Look carefully at the map. How many other changes will be made necessary by the Chadwick bypass?

2   Use the maps to make two papier mâché models of the valley, one as the valley is now, and the second showing the completed bypass.

3   Can you think of another possible route for the bypass? How many problems will your new route solve? Will it bring any others? Remember: a longer bypass will be more expensive to build.

71

Protests

This letter's to say

Dear Sir or Madam,
This letter's to say
Your property
Stands bang in the way
Of Progress, and
Will be knocked down
On March the third
At half-past one.

There is no appeal,
Since the National Need
Depends on more
And still more Speed,
And this, in turn,
Dear Sir or Madam,
Depends on half England
Being tar-macadam.
(But your house will —
We are pleased to say —
Be the fastest lane
Of the Motorway).

Meanwhile the Borough
Corporation
Offer you new
Accommodation
Three miles away
On the thirteenth floor
(Flat Number Q 6824).

But please take note,
The Council regret:
No dog, cat, bird
Or other pet;
No noise permitted,
No singing in the bath
(For permits to drink
Or smoke or laugh
Apply on Form Z 327);
No children admitted
Aged under eleven;
No hawkers, tramps
Or roof-top lunchers;
No opening doors
To Bible-punchers.

Failure to pay
Your rent, when due,
Will lead to our
Evicting you.
The Council demand
That you consent
To the terms above
When you pay your rent.

Meanwhile we hope
You will feel free
To consult us
Should there prove to be
The slightest case
Of difficulty.

With kind regards,
Yours faithfully . . .
Raymond Wilson

1 What reasons are given for the demolition of the property? Do you think they are good reasons?
2 Suppose you received a letter like this. How would you feel? How would the demolition of your home change your life?
3 The letter says there is no appeal against the decision. Do you think this is true? Is there any way the householder could try to prevent his home being demolished?
4 Imagine you are the householder. Write a reply protesting at the way you are being treated.
5 Write a poem about the demolition of your home. Say how you feel as you leave it for the last time, and watch it reduced to rubble.

Changes in Your Area

1 Are there any buildings in your area about to be demolished? If so, take photographs of them before demolition. Afterwards take photographs of whatever replaces them.
   Record the opinions of local people about these changes. Try to find people who can tell you their memories of the old buildings.
2 Make your own *Changes* booklet recording such changes in your area. Old photographs are fascinating, especially if they show buildings which can still be recognised. Try to take photographs of the same place now. Sometimes it is impossible. It might require standing in the middle of a bypass!
3 How many of these changes are for the better? How many are not? Try to give reasons for your conclusions.

A Public Inquiry

A public inquiry is arranged for members of the Chadwick community to give their views in an open meeting. As you can see there are many points of view.

Farmer Johnson: "The bypass will cut right through my farm. It will be a disaster!"

Mrs. Williams, teacher: "I can't wait for the bypass. It will mean safer road crossing for the children, and I won't have to shout above the traffic to make myself heard."

Ben Morris, garage proprietor: "Most of my custom comes from the traffic passing through Chadwick. I shall go out of business."

Madge Dawson, cafe proprietor: "Without the lorry drivers I don't see how I can manage."

Abdul Haziz, schoolboy: "They promised us an adventure playground in the conservation area, but the bypass will spoil that."

Les Harrison, lorry driver: "I travel through Chadwick about six times a week. The bypass will save me hours."

James Macgregor, archaeologist: "We have discovered some priceless historical remains near the derelict cottage. Construction of a bypass will destroy them."

Sally Holmes, naturalist: "We have three species of wild flower in our proposed conservation area. They must be protected."

Councillor Geraldine Pierce: "The bypass will save the town centre, making it a quiet, safe and pleasant place to shop in."

Let each member of your group take the role of one of these people to speak at the public inquiry. If you prefer you could play the role of a Chadwick resident or shopkeeper.

Before the Inquiry

a) Study the map of the proposed bypass and assess how its construction will affect you. Can you think of an alternative route for the bypass, or other ways of easing the congestion in Chadwick centre?

Can you think of solutions to some of the problems and fears expressed above?

b) Make careful notes of what you will say at the inquiry.

c) Write a letter to the local newspaper expressing your views and ideas. By doing so you may win a great deal of support for your views in advance of the inquiry.

d) Get together with others who share your viewpoint and prepare posters and handouts to rally further support.

e) Write an essay entitled "A Bypass for Chadwick?"
   1 Introduction: State what you are writing about. Explain briefly why a bypass is being considered.
   2 First main paragraph: Write about the advantages a bypass would bring to Chadwick.
   3 Second main paragraph: Write about the problems a bypass would bring.
   4 Conclusion: Say what you think should be done, with reasons for your decision.

At the Inquiry

A chairman will give everyone a chance to speak in turn. When all the different viewpoints have been heard, take a vote to decide if the bypass should go ahead.

New Words

In Unit 2 we looked at how the English language developed from the language spoken by the Anglo-Saxons. In this unit we have seen how the same people settled as farmers. Can you guess what these Anglo-Saxon words have become in modern English?

> feld   treow   kye   spada

As our language developed new words were needed for new discoveries, inventions and ideas.

New Meanings

Sometimes old words were given new meanings. Broadcasting once meant to scatter seeds by hand, but with the invention of radio it gained its present meaning. Use your dictionary to find the original and new meanings of these words:

> plastic   record   disc   tape   film   plug   earth   battery

Compound Words

Sometimes new words were made by joining two words together to make a compound word. Examples are:

> newspaper   skyscraper   streamline   bypass   hovercraft

How many others can you think of?

Borrowing from Other Languages

English has always borrowed words from other languages. Here are some examples:

> garage   chauffeur   goulash   mango   camouflage   shampoo
> ombudsman   casserole   grenade   denim   quartz   encore

Use a dictionary which gives the origins of words to complete this chart for each of the words above.

English word	Meaning	Origin	Original word and meaning
garage	a building where motor vehicles are stored or repaired	French	garer — to secure

Words from Names

Many common words come from people's names.
The word *cardigan* was named after Lord Cardigan. *Wellington boots,* or wellies, are named after the Duke of Wellington.
Use a dictionary and an encyclopedia to complete the chart for each of these words.

> mackintosh   bunsen   watt   ampere   volt   sandwich   diesel
> tarmac (adam)   listerine   pasteurised (milk)

Word	Name	Origin
wellington	Duke of Wellington	Wore rubber knee boots

Words from Science

As new discoveries were made in science new words were required to explain them. As we have already seen some words came from the names of people, such as watt and volt, while occasionally older words like earth and battery were given new meanings.

Yet the vast majority of scientific words that have passed into general use have come from Latin or Greek. Words like *telephone* and *telegram* use the prefix *tele-* which means "far".

1 Write down as many words as you can which begin with the prefix *tele-*. Can you explain how each word came about?
2 Do the same with words beginning with *photo-* (from the Greek for "light".)
3 Use a dictionary with word origins to explain these words from science. The first one has been done for you.
   a) capsule — from the Latin word *capsa* (box) and *capsula* (small box). b) satellite
   c) astronaut d) orbit e) computer f) electric g) stereophonic h) video

Acronyms

Laser is an acronym of "**L**ight **A**mplification by **S**timulated **E**mission of **R**adiation". What do you think an acronym is?

Radar is another acronym. Can you find out the words it came from? Incidentally, the word "radar" is also a palindrome. What is a palindrome? Where does the word come from? How many palindromes can you think of?

The word *posh* has an interesting history. In the days of long voyages to the East by sailing boat the important passengers always had cabins which allowed the prevailing wind to cool their cabins. This meant they travelled "**P**ort **O**ut, **S**tarboard **H**ome".

The initial letters of the names of organisations are often used as words. Find out what these names stand for: NATO, UNESCO, BAFTA, MORI, NASA, OXFAM.

Slang

Slang is language which is not usually accepted as polite English. It comes from attempts to bring fresh expressions into spoken English. Most slang words are short lived: they become dulled with use and fall out of fashion.

How many of these examples of outdated schoolboy slang do you hear used today:

spiffing, smashing, fab, fantabulous, ginormous?

What do you think these words mean? Which words do you think the last two have come from?

Make a list of slang words used by children of your own age, together with a meaning for each one. Can you explain the origin of any of them?

A few slang words do make their way into Standard English. Believe it or not these words were once slang words: *fun, flimsy, enthusiasm, nervous, fuss* and *extra*.

Are there any slang words you use which you think may one day be accepted as Standard English? Give a reason for your answer.

Rhyming Slang

"Whistle and flute" is Cockney rhyming slang for "suit". What do you think these are: plates of meat, Rosy Lee, titfer or tit-for-tat, trouble and strife, bees and honey?

Back Slang

Back slang was used as a secret language by street traders in the middle of the nineteenth century. "Yob" is back slang for "boy". Write back slang for the numbers one to ten.

Make a list of any other rhyming slang and back slang expressions you can find.

A World Language?

Today English is spoken by one person in every ten across the globe. In countries such as the U.S.A., Canada, Australia and New Zealand, where many English speaking people settled in previous centuries, it is a first language. In many other countries English is a very important second language.

American English

When the first English speakers settled in North America in the seventeenth century they took with them seventeenth century English, which is not the English we speak today. From that point American English developed and changed in different ways from the language in Britain.

Sometimes the differences were because Americans kept seventeenth century words and constructions which later changed in Britain. Examples of these are "fall" for "autumn", "platter" for "plate" and "gotten" for "got".

New words came into American English because of borrowing from the American Indians. These were needed to describe the new things they found there: canoe, bluff, watershed, raccoon, skunk and possum. New phrases came from the same source: play possum, go on the warpath and bury the hatchet. Other words came from settlers from other countries: barbecue, chocolate and tomato from Spanish settlers, gopher and chowder from French, coleslaw, cookie, landscape, snoop and spook from Dutch settlers.

In 1828 Noah Webster published an "American Dictionary of the English Language" with new spellings such as "color" for "colour" and "traveler" for "traveller". How many more American spellings of English words do you know?

American English began to use different words too: candy for sweets, apartment for flat, faucet for tap, truck for lorry, railroad for railway and elevator for lift. How many more can you find?

Canadian English

Since the U.S.A. and Canada are such close neighbours it is understandable that Canadian English is similar to American English. However there are differences. The Canadians retain the word "tap" instead of "faucet", but use truck for lorry and gas for petrol. They have adopted some American spellings, e.g. tire, wagon, aluminum, but retain the original English spellings of some words, e.g. theatre, colour and woollen.

Australian English

Australia had many animals unique to the continent and early settlers borrowed their names from the Aborigines, e.g. kangaroo, wombat and budgerigar. They borrowed other words too: billabong (waterhole) and boomerang.

A World Language?

Because English is spoken so widely across the world it is a useful link amongst people of different races and religions, but could it ever become a world language?

A number of things make English a difficult language to learn. One is the number of words it contains. The Oxford Dictionary lists half a million English words, while German has only 185,000 and French fewer than 100,000. A second difficulty is English spelling — a problem for British people too! A third problem is the way the language continues to change and develop differently in each place it is spoken.

Yet the advantage of using English as an international language of world trade will probably continue as long as satellites, television and telephones make world communication possible.

To write about

1 In what ways did American English change differently from English in Britain?
2 What effect did the publication of Webster's dictionary have on written American English? Give a few examples.
3 Explain in your own words some of the differences and similarities between Canadian and American English.
4 Explain in your own words the problems foreigners face when learning English.

Words, Words, Words

Synonyms

The English language has about half a million words. Most of these words are synonyms: words close in meaning to other words. Having such a variety of words to choose from makes it possible for us to select the exact word we need.

A thesaurus is a special word-finding dictionary which gives lists of such synonyms, and writers make extensive use of one when they are stuck for a precise word.

Look at this extract from *Collins Thesaurus*.

waddle rock, shuffle, sway, toddle, totter, wobble

wade 1. ford, paddle, splash, walk through 2. *With* **through** drudge, labour, peg away, plough through, toil, work one's way 3. *With* **in** *or* **into** assail, attack, get stuck in (*Sl.*), go for, launch oneself at, light into (*Inf.*), set about, tackle, tear into (*Inf.*)

waffle 1. *v.* blather, jabber, prate, prattle, rabbit on (*Brit. sl.*), verbalize, witter on (*Inf.*) 2. *n.* blather, jabber, padding, prating, prattle, prolixity, verbiage, verbosity, wordiness

waft 1. *v.* bear, be carried, carry, convey, drift, float, ride, transmit, transport 2. *n.* breath, breeze, current, draught, puff, whiff

wag[1] 1. *v.* bob, flutter, nod, oscillate, quiver, rock, shake, stir, vibrate, waggle, wave, wiggle 2. *n.* bob, flutter, nod, oscillation, quiver, shake, toss, vibration, waggle, wave, wiggle

wag[2] *n.* card (*Inf.*), clown, comedian, comic, humorist, jester, joker, wit

wage 1. *n. Also* **wages** allowance, compensation, earnings, emolument, fee, hire, pay, payment, recompense, remuneration ...

wait 1. *v.* abide, bide one's time, cool one's heels, dally, delay, hang fire, hold back, hold on (*Inf.*), linger, mark time, pause, remain, rest, stand by, stay, tarry 2. *n.* delay, halt, hold-up, interval, pause, rest, stay

waiter, waitress attendant, server, steward, stewardess

wait on *or* **upon** attend, minister to, serve, tend

waive abandon, defer, dispense with, forgo, give up, postpone, put off, refrain from, relinquish, remit, renounce, resign, set aside, surrender

waiver abandonment, abdication, disclaimer, giving up, relinquishment, remission, renunciation, resignation, setting aside, surrender

wake[1] *v.* 1. arise, awake, awaken, bestir, come to, get up, rouse, rouse from sleep, stir 2. activate, animate, arouse, awaken, enliven, excite, fire, galvanize, kindle, provoke, quicken, stimulate, stir up ~*n.* 3. deathwatch, funeral, vigil, watch

wake[2] aftermath, backwash, path, track, trail, train, wash, waves

wakeful 1. ... restless, sleep...

1 Write down three synonyms for each of these words: *waft, wag, waddle.*

2 Look at the synonyms for *wake.* Do they all have exactly the same meaning? Choose three and write a sentence for each one showing its precise meaning.

3 Why are there two entries for *wag* and *wake*?

4 Complete these sentences with a suitable word from the listings for *wag.*
 a) The building began to _____ when the first shock of the earthquake hit it.
 b) Mrs. Larby _____ her finger at the two children.
 c) Billy Bannerman is a _____ on television.
 d) He _____ his head in agreement.
 e) The boat _____ like a cork on the water.
 f) When the motor was switched on the metal began to _____.
 g) The butterfly _____ its wings.
 h) She began to _____ with fear.

Spelling

We have said that English spelling is a problem for everyone, whether native English speakers or not. It is perhaps a good time to remind ourselves of a useful way to learn the spelling of a difficult word. It is the Look, Cover, Write and Check method:

> LOOK at the word and say it to yourself.
> COVER it, close your eyes and see the word in your mind.
> WRITE out the spelling.
> CHECK it. If it is wrong then repeat the above stages.

Try it for yourself on these words.

procession	ceremony	associate	discussion	accompany
committee	preparation	immediately	suspicious	manageable

Mad Meals
Grilled cork
Matchbox on toast
glass soup
roasted clock
ping-pong ball and chips
Acorn sandwich
fillet of calculator
trouser salad
grilled lamp-post
ice-cream (vanilla, soap or pepper)
Michael Rosen

1 What a lot of mad meals Michael Rosen has dreamed up!
Write your own poem of "junk" foods. You could use Michael Rosen's poem as a model if you like, e.g.

> Grilled _____
> _____ on toast
> _____ soup
> etc.

Alternatively why not use your own ideas? Try to find different ways food could be cooked, e.g. casseroled, broiled, fried, barbecued, etc.

2 Write a zany recipe for Scrap Heap Casserole.

3 Write a mad menu for the "Round the Twist Restaurant".

Spoonerisms

William Archibald Spooner was once Warden of New College, Oxford. He is famous for his "spoonerisms", phrases in which the first letters of some words are interchanged, e.g. "shoving leopard" for "loving shepherd".

1 When announcing a hymn he once said, "Kinquering Congs their titles take."
What do you think he meant to say?

2 What do you think these people meant to say?

For real enjoyment, give me a well-boiled icycle!

What a gritty pearl!

I have just received a blushing crow.

3 Write the following correctly.
"Sir, you have tasted two whole worms; you have hissed all my mystery lectures and have been caught fighting a liar in the quad; you will leave by the next town drain."

4 Can you think of any spoonerisms of your own?

A Found Poem

A found poem is written using names, words or phrases that have been found in print or heard in everyday speech. The poet collects them and then decides which to use.

Why not write your own found poem? Look in a telephone directory for interesting names. Use alliteration (names beginning with the same sound), rhyme and rhythm to make your found poem interesting. Here are two lines to start you off:

> Shaylor, Shepherd, Shannon, Shires,
> Milligan, Mulligan Murphy, Myers.

Other sources of material for found poems are place names (maps and atlases), advertising slogans (TV, radio and magazines), radio and TV programme titles (programme listings), everyday sayings (anyone you listen to), pop group names, animal names, etc. etc.

What Do They Really Mean?

1. Rewrite the words of each speaker to show what they really mean.
2. Which of the above is an example of a spoonerism?
3. Which speakers use idioms?
4. "You won't get nothing for Christmas" really means "You will get something for Christmas". This is not at all what the speaker intended. Rewrite the following so that they mean what the speaker intends:—
   a) I didn't do nothing.
   b) She couldn't do nothing right.
5. We learned in Level 4 that a malapropism is an amusing misuse of a word. Which of the above is a malapropism?
6. Irony is when the words used seem to mean one thing, but the real meaning is the very opposite. Which of the above is an example of irony?
7. The words of the girl in picture 6 are ambiguous, i.e. they could have four different meanings. Think of why dad was angry. Write sentences showing two possible meanings. Do the same with these.
   a) Jenny took the book from Anthea and drove off in her car.
   b) In the morning I had coffee with John who told very funny jokes and spent the afternoon shopping.

Writing Sentences

A Write these sentences in the shortest possible way. The first one has been done for you.

1 The lady lost a ring which was valuable.
The lady lost a valuable ring.

2 A medal was presented to the boy who had shown bravery.
3 The man drove his car to the garage and parked his car on the forecourt.
4 The man who was injured was knocked down by a passing car.
5 The people who clean our school have asked for an increase in their wages.
6 As soon as the sun rose the men who were going fishing set off.

B Do the same with these, but think carefully first.

1 None of the men was unfit.
2 It is not true that John is not in.
3 There wasn't anyone who wanted not to have a dinner.
4 You are not allowed not to attend swimming lessons.

C Change the underlined words to give each sentence its opposite meaning.

1 He will <u>arrive</u> this afternoon.
2 The boy was <u>miserable</u>.
3 He <u>seldom</u> plays football.
4 The tomb contained an <u>immense</u> amount of treasure.
5 Sara made a <u>rapid</u> recovery from her illness.
6 The landslide <u>concealed</u> the cave entrance.
7 Her new dress was extremely <u>expensive</u>.
8 He <u>purchased</u> a very rare book.

D Change the underlined word in each sentence above, but without changing the meaning.

E Add a prefix to give each of these words an opposite meaning. Put each of the words you have made into a sentence of your own.

un-	in-	im-	mis-	ab-	dis-

a) behave **b)** kind **c)** pure **d)** visible **e)** patient
f) normal **g)** connect **h)** wise **i)** content **j)** polite

F Change the following into reported speech. The first one has been done for you.

1 "There will be a delivery at two o'clock," the shopkeeper told him.

The shopkeeper told him there would be a delivery at two o'clock.

2 "Where are you going?" Gemma asked Pat.
3 "Don't open it!" he warned her.
4 "What time is the next train?" Lynn asked the porter.
5 "It's due in exactly eight minutes," he replied.
6 "I've got to go now," Paul said, "but I shall be back tomorrow."

G Change the following into direct speech.

1 Jim said that he had finished all his work.
2 Sally asked Peter if he had seen her pen.
3 Mother ordered Robert to open the door that minute.
4 Sue begged Don to tell her where he had hidden her books.
5 She told the removal man to take great care of her valuable Chinese vase.
6 She warned Zoe not to believe a word Tony said.

Past and Future Time

The future tense of a verb is made by putting *shall* or *will* before the main verb.
We use *shall* with *I* and *we*. We use *will* with *you, he, she, it* and *they*.

> I shall go. You will go.
> We shall work. They will work.

In speech these have
shortened forms.

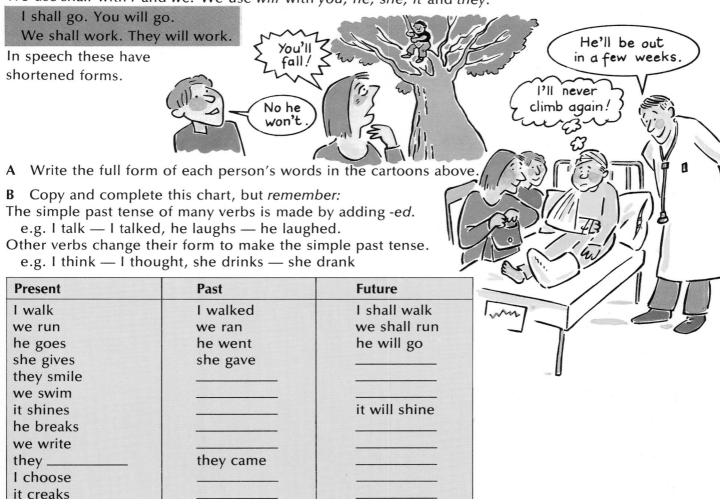

A Write the full form of each person's words in the cartoons above.

B Copy and complete this chart, but *remember:*
The simple past tense of many verbs is made by adding *-ed.*
  e.g. I talk — I talked, he laughs — he laughed.
Other verbs change their form to make the simple past tense.
  e.g. I think — I thought, she drinks — she drank

Present	Past	Future
I walk	I walked	I shall walk
we run	we ran	we shall run
he goes	he went	he will go
she gives	she gave	_____
they smile	_____	_____
we swim	_____	_____
it shines	_____	it will shine
he breaks	_____	_____
we write	_____	_____
they _____	they came	_____
I choose	_____	_____
it creaks	_____	_____

C Write each sentence. Put the future tense of the verb in brackets in the space.
1 The bell _____ at three o'clock.   (ring)
2 I _____ the ceiling.   (paint)
3 Cathy _____ two hours late.   (is)
4 We _____ hockey later this afternoon.   (play)
5 They _____ at about six o'clock.   (arrive)

D Rewrite this passage as if it has already happened.
Begin like this:

> Sue took her time having her breakfast . . .

Sue takes her time having her breakfast, which makes her brother extremely impatient. He
stamps about grumbling. Eventually he decides to go without her. He puts on his coat and leaves
the house. He runs down the street and catches the bus with seconds to spare.

E Rewrite the same passage as if it is yet to happen.
Begin like this:

> Sue will take her time having her breakfast . . .

New Tales for Old

These two rhymes are amusing variations of traditional nursery rhymes. Look closely at the changes that have been made.

Humpty Dumpty sat on a wall,
Humpty Dumpty had a great fall.
All the king's horses and all the king's men
Had scrambled eggs for breakfast again.
    Anon.

Mary had a jaguar,
It's teeth were sharp and bright,
And everywhere she took her pet
It gave the boys a fright.

The "Humpty Dumpty" verse is identical to the original except for the last line, which comes as a surprise.

The verse about Mary's pet is based more loosely on "Mary had a little lamb". The changes begin with the very first line, but the rhythm is immediately recognisable.

Make up your own new nursery rhyme
If you prefer you may begin by experimenting with new versions of the rhymes above: a new last line for Humpty Dumpty, for example, or a different, but unusual, pet for Mary.

Make a list of other nursery rhymes which might be suitable for changing. Select one and think about how you might change it most effectively. Your verse won't be very long, so spend most of your time planning and experimenting.

Traditional Stories
In his *Revolting Rhymes* Roald Dahl has made some fascinating changes to traditional tales. Here is an extract from one of them.

1 What changes has Roald Dahl made?

2 Did you find any of these changes amusing? Why?

3 Do you prefer this version to the original? Why?

4 In what way is Red Riding Hood different from the way she is portrayed in the original? Do you think this makes her a more interesting character? Why do you think so?

In came the little girl in red.
She stopped. She stared. And then she said,
"What great big ears you have, Grandma."
"All the better to hear you with," the Wolf replied.
"What great big eyes you have, Grandma,"
   said Little Red Riding Hood.
"All the better to see you with," the Wolf replied.
He sat there watching her and smiled.
He thought, I'm going to eat this child.
Compared with her old Grandmamma
She's going to taste like caviare.
Then Little Red Riding Hood said, *"But Grandma,
what a lovely great big furry coat you have on."*
"That's wrong!" cried Wolf. "Have you forgot
"To tell me what BIG TEETH I've got?
"Ah well, no matter what you say,
"I'm going to eat you anyway."
The small girl smiles. One eyelid flickers.
She whips a pistol from her knickers.
She aims it at the creature's head
And *bang bang bang*, she shoots him dead.
A few weeks later, in the wood,
I came across Miss Riding Hood.
But what a change! No cloak of red,
No silly hood upon her head.
She said, "Hello, and do please note
"My lovely furry WOLFSKIN COAT."
(From *Revolting Rhymes* by Roald Dahl)

Brave Princess, Gentle Knight

To think and talk about

1 Make a list of fairy tales and other traditional stories. Who are the heroes of these stories? Are there any heroines?
2 Make a list of words to describe a) the men, b) the women, in these stories.
3 Compare the two lists. What do you notice about the way men and women are treated in such stories? Why do you think this is?
4 Think about men and women in real life. Are there any qualities in your lists which are confined to either men or women?

The Wrestling Princess
Read this extract from *The Wrestling Princess* by Judy Corbalis.

Once upon a time there was a princess who was six feet tall, who liked her own way and who loved to wrestle. Every day, she would challenge the guards at her father's palace to wrestling matches and every day, she won. Then she would pick up the loser and fling him on the ground, but gently, because she had a very kind nature.

The princess had one other unusual hobby. She liked to drive forklift trucks. Because she was a princess, and her father was very rich, she had three forklift trucks of her own — a blue one, a yellow one, and a green and purple striped one with a coronet on each side. Whenever there was a royal parade, the king would ride in front in his golden carriage, behind him would ride a company of soldiers and behind them came the princess driving her striped royal forklift truck. The king got very cross about it but the princess simply said, "If I can't drive my forklift truck, I won't go," and because she was such a good wrestler, the king was too scared to disagree with her.

(From *The Wrestling Princess* by Judy Corbalis)

1 Did you enjoy this extract? Can you say why?
2 How is the princess in this story different from princesses in traditional tales?
3 Do you think a princess may be just as brave as a prince? Why?
4 Continue the story of the wrestling princess. What adventures might she have?

A Picture Book for Children
Write your own traditional story with a twist, especially for a younger child. Talk to him/her and find out what sort of story he would like to read. Keep your story simple, like the one here which has been written using a computer program called "Fairy Tales". The program allows colour graphics to be printed, but of course you may draw your own pictures if you prefer.

Once upon a time a dragon began to eat hundreds of people. Then Debbie Dobkins said, "Leave the dragon to me!"

UNIT 6   A Better World?

From Alpha-B75-Earth Visitors' Guide
Seen through a telescope,
You may think,
Earth a lovely planet.
Alphan travellers are warned,
This is pure deception.
Earth is tricky,
In places, toxic,
And earth-dwellers
Are not to be trusted,
Being primitive and untamed
Members of the galaxy;
Violent polluters
Of their biosphere.
Earth is as bizarre a planet,
As any in the universe.
John Cunliffe

A
The poem is the poet's way of making us stop and think what we are doing to our planet. But what exactly are we doing? The following passage gives an introduction to the problems of pollution. Read it carefully to find the answers to these questions.

1   What are pesticides?
2   What is acid rain?
3   Name two ways in which man is destroying the world's forests.
4   How does the loss of forests upset the balance of nature?
5   Explain in your own words what the "greenhouse effect" is.
6   How do we pollute our rivers?

Pollution
Few people today would deny that we have a higher standard of living than at any time in the past. Yet this higher standard of living has been achieved at a terrible cost. Progress has brought with it changes to our environment. Man has upset the balance of nature on this planet by polluting its land, water and air.

Pollution of the Air
With the Industrial Revolution of the early 1700s came smoke from factory chimneys poisoning the air of the growing towns and cities. Although there are fewer such chimneys now, our air is daily polluted by the exhaust fumes of cars and lorries.

When polluted air mixes with rain water it produces an acid which attacks metal, wood, brick and stone. Forests of trees wither and die from this acid rain. Plants grow more slowly and are less healthy. This in turn affects the animals which eat them.

Pollution of the Land
Today's farmers use large amounts of pesticides which kill not only pests but sometimes they kill harmless insects too. The birds which eat pests with pesticides in them are also affected. Some of these birds are in turn eaten by birds of prey which later die from the poison.

In some countries vast areas of forest are burned to make the land available for pasture or crops. The forest plants and animals then die as their natural habitat is

British Steel V

destroyed. For a short time the newly cleared land is fertile from the ashes of the burned forest, but soon the soil becomes poor and more forest has to be cleared. The abandoned land then begins to erode and blow away as dust.

The burning of forests has another effect. Tree are great plant factories, changing carbon dioxide into oxygen. As the forests disappear less carbon dioxide is converted into oxygen. This is happening at a time when the industrialised nations are burning fuel at an increasing rate and so filling the atmosphere with its by-product, carbon dioxide. Consequently there is a gradual build-up of carbon dioxide in the upper atmosphere. This allows the sun's heat to pass through, but at the same time it is trapped so that the Earth slowly warms up. This is known as the "greenhouse effect". If it continues it will have disastrous effects on climate.

Water Pollution

About one third of our drinking water comes from rivers, but many rivers are polluted with sewage and industrial waste or pesticides washed off the land by rain water. In some rivers all fish and most plants have been killed off. Eventually such pollution is washed out to sea, spreading the deadly effects still further.

The widespread pollution of our planet must be stopped. We must allow nature to restore its balance, before it is too late. The survival of the human race may depend upon it.

Deforestation in the Amazon

B Now you have read the passage, read the poem again and answer these questions.
1 Where is the Earth toxic?
2 In what ways might an alien civilisation see us as "primitive and untamed"?
3 Why is Earth described as a *bizarre* planet?

C To think and talk about
1 The passage describes some of the problems of pollution. Can you think of other ways in which man pollutes the environment?
2 Can you think of any solutions to the problems of pollution?
3 Is there anything you could do now to reduce pollution?
4 Is there anything you would like to do when you are older?

Planet Earth

Write a reply to this letter accepting the producer's invitation. Discuss with your group where you will find the information you need. Decide how best to share the research among your group. When you have made your notes, hold another meeting to discuss your findings.

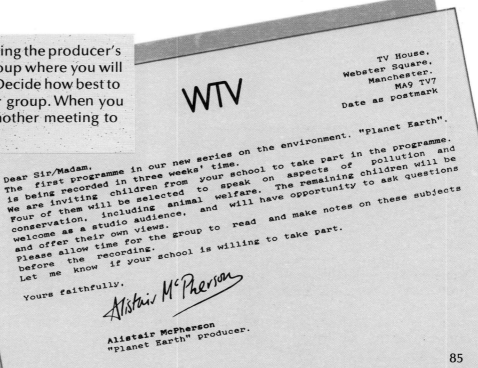

WTV

TV House,
Webster Square,
Manchester.
MA9 TV7
Date as postmark

Dear Sir/Madam,

The first programme in our new series on the environment, "Planet Earth", is being recorded in three weeks' time.

We are inviting children from your school to take part in the programme. Four of them will be selected to speak on aspects of pollution and conservation, including animal welfare. The remaining children will be welcome as a studio audience, and will have opportunity to ask questions and offer their own views.

Please allow time for the group to read and make notes on these subjects before the recording.

Let me know if your school is willing to take part.

Yours faithfully,

Alistair McPherson

Alistair McPherson
"Planet Earth" producer.

Pollution

Professor Farleigh is giving a lecture on the subject of pollution. He has written notes and these have become mixed up.
Sort them out into subjects, and then put the notes for each subject into their correct order.

a
- Bacteria acts upon the treated sewage to break it down harmlessly, but if it is poured into the rivers untreated then the bacteria cannot cope.
- When the bacteria cannot do their job properly the river becomes polluted. Fish and plants die and the water may carry disease.
- The polluted river water is then carried to the sea which will in its turn become polluted.

b
- Water pollution is just as devastating.
- Just as we need air to live, so we cannot survive without clean water. In our country we are lucky to have a plentiful supply, but a good deal of this is wasted because it is unfit to drink.
- One third of our drinking water comes from rivers which are also used to dispose of sewage and industrial waste.
- Most of the sewage and waste is treated before it goes into the rivers.

c
- Introduction: what pollution means and where it comes from.
- Pollution means to spoil something by making it foul and poisonous.
- There are many different types of pollution from different sources, the most common being air pollution and water pollution.

d
- As well as making our breathing difficult, air pollution has other damaging effects: it fades paint on buildings, brickwork is eaten away, plant growth is stunted and trees die.

e
- In our homes and factories fuels such as oil and coal are used. They give off smoke which pollutes the air.
- Even in areas where smokeless fuels are used, or where there are chimneys with filters to trap gases and soot, air pollution still exists because one of its main causes is the motor car.
- Cars use petrol in their engines and when this fuel is burnt, poisonous fumes are created. These pollute the air we breathe.

Look back at your re-ordered notes for Professor Farleigh's lecture. Use them to answer these questions.

1   How does Professor Farleigh define pollution?
2   Which two specific kinds of pollution does Professor Farleigh concentrate on?
3   What does the professor see as one of the main contributors to air pollution?
4   What steps have been taken to control air pollution in certain areas?
5   How much of our drinking water is taken from rivers which also receive industrial waste and sewage?
6   What job is done by the bacteria already present in the river?
7   What will happen to the sea if we allow all our rivers to become polluted?

Making Notes
Here are some of the notes Rachel made about the lecture. Notice how she has written down only the important words, and has not used complete sentences.

Lecture : Pollution by Professor Farleigh

Pollution : to spoil something by making foul/poisonous. Many types ; air, water most common.

Air - need for life
Fuels : oil, coal → make smoke → pollute air
Smokeless fuel and chimneys with filters help, but cars still a problem.

Petrol — poisonous fumes

Make your own notes, like Rachel's, about the rest of the lecture.

Fish in a Polluted River
His mother's dead. And now his aunt
Says, 'Where's the purifying plant?
He cannot breathe, he cannot swim
Because of what you've done to him.'
Ian Serraillier

To think and talk about
1   Read this poem carefully. How does it make you feel? Why? What do you think can or should be done about river pollution?
2   What do you think the "purifying plant" is?
3   Discuss the "domino effect": the effect of the death of one life form on other forms of life.

What a Load of Rubbish!

What Happens to Our Rubbish?

It has been estimated that each person in Britain, on average, throws away 159 kg of rubbish every year, and this figure does not take into account large items such as used cars, fridges, mattresses, etc. We accept rubbish as part of our daily lives, but what happens to it once the dustman has taken it away?

At one time a huge pit would have been dug and all the rubbish dropped in. Then the site would have been covered with earth and the rubbish left to rot. Unfortunately this method of waste disposal is only suitable for those items of rubbish which do rot, such as food scraps, natural fabrics and paper. Much of today's rubbish consists of metals and plastic which do not rot, so alternative methods of disposal have had to be found.

Re-cycling is now an important part of waste disposal. Modern living consumes much of the natural, valuable materials of our planet, and ways have been found to salvage waste material so that it can be re-used.

First refuse trucks bring the waste to the re-cycling plant where it is tipped into huge bunkers. Conveyor belts carry this waste material into the main building where workers sort through it for glass bottles and jars. These are passed to the bottle store where they are ground down and sent to be re-moulded into new bottles and jars.

The remainder of the waste continues along the conveyor belts passing huge magnets which extract the tins and other metal objects. These are then graded so that they may be re-formed into new metal products. More conveyor belts are used and other teams of workers pick out the other re-usable materials. Paper and card are re-used to make cardboard boxes or newspaper after their re-cycling process. Rubber can also be re-formed, and rags and bones may be re-cycled as paper, glue and even postage stamps.

What is left on the conveyor belt after all this "picking" has been done is either bio-degradable waste, such as foodscraps, which will eventually rot away, or combustible waste which can be disposed of in an incinerator.

Activities

1 Use the passage to help you complete this flow chart showing how rubbish is sorted for re-cycling.

2 Fill in a chart like this one to show the different kinds of rubbish that is put into your classroom bin in one week. Think about how this rubbish could be re-used. How would you re-cycle food waste? Ask your teacher for activity sheets **5.6a** and **5.6b** for some practical ideas on how to make good use of your rubbish.

Refuse trucks empty contents into bunker.

▼

Rubbish on conveyor belts to main building.

▼

Glass bottles and jars sorted ▷ Ground dow to make new bottles

▼

Rubbish Collection chart

Rubbish	Mon.	Tue.	Wed.	Thur.	Fri.	TOTAL
Paper (bags etc.)	I	II	I			
Newspapers	II		I			
Plastic containers (tubs)	I		I			
Glass containers		I				
Food scraps	III	IIII	II			
Metal cans etc.	I	I	II			
Other plastic (bags, film)	II	II	I			
Other paper and card	I					
Others			I			

How an Incinerator Works

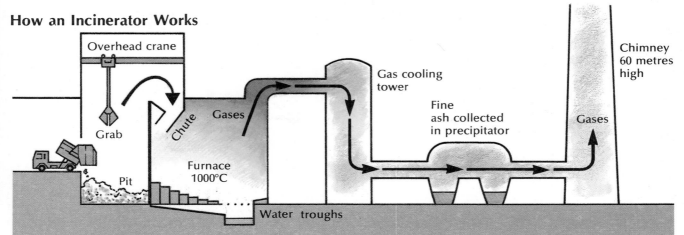

Study this diagram carefully. Write a detailed description of how an incinerator works.

To think and talk about
Burning rubbish may seem an easy solution to the problem of waste disposal, but can you think of any other pollution problems burning might bring? Discuss these with your group. How do you think such problems can be solved?

Litter
Litter is one of the most common forms of pollution, and one of the most unsightly. Yet it is unnecessary. Councils spend thousands of pounds on litter bins, but many people simply do not bother to use them. Such unthinking behaviour results not only in untidy streets, but in danger to people and to wild life.

Activities

1 Study these photographs carefully. For each one say how the litter is dangerous and what the consequences might be.
2 What other dangerous litter can you think of?
3 Make a dramatic warning poster showing how litter can be dangerous.
4 Make your own notes on rubbish and re-cycling for use in the *Planet Earth* T.V. programme.

Tree Poems
Look at this poem about waste. It consists of five lines, each containing a specified number of syllables:

Line 1: One syllable
Line 2: Two syllables
Line 3: Three syllables
Line 4: Four syllables
Line 5: One syllable

Waste,
Litter,
In the street,
Swirling about,
Mess!

It is called a tree poem because when it is written down it takes on the shape of a fir tree. Tree poems may be written on any subject.

1 Write your own tree poem about an aspect of pollution.
2 Write a tree poem on a different subject.

89

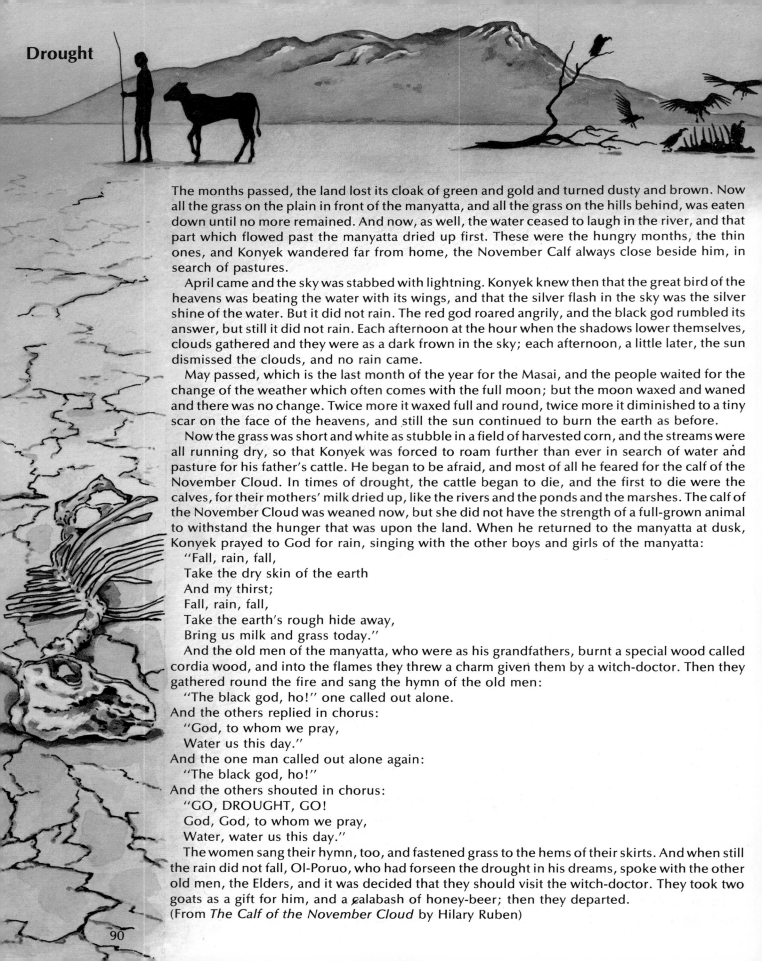

Drought

The months passed, the land lost its cloak of green and gold and turned dusty and brown. Now all the grass on the plain in front of the manyatta, and all the grass on the hills behind, was eaten down until no more remained. And now, as well, the water ceased to laugh in the river, and that part which flowed past the manyatta dried up first. These were the hungry months, the thin ones, and Konyek wandered far from home, the November Calf always close beside him, in search of pastures.

April came and the sky was stabbed with lightning. Konyek knew then that the great bird of the heavens was beating the water with its wings, and that the silver flash in the sky was the silver shine of the water. But it did not rain. The red god roared angrily, and the black god rumbled its answer, but still it did not rain. Each afternoon at the hour when the shadows lower themselves, clouds gathered and they were as a dark frown in the sky; each afternoon, a little later, the sun dismissed the clouds, and no rain came.

May passed, which is the last month of the year for the Masai, and the people waited for the change of the weather which often comes with the full moon; but the moon waxed and waned and there was no change. Twice more it waxed full and round, twice more it diminished to a tiny scar on the face of the heavens, and still the sun continued to burn the earth as before.

Now the grass was short and white as stubble in a field of harvested corn, and the streams were all running dry, so that Konyek was forced to roam further than ever in search of water and pasture for his father's cattle. He began to be afraid, and most of all he feared for the calf of the November Cloud. In times of drought, the cattle began to die, and the first to die were the calves, for their mothers' milk dried up, like the rivers and the ponds and the marshes. The calf of the November Cloud was weaned now, but she did not have the strength of a full-grown animal to withstand the hunger that was upon the land. When he returned to the manyatta at dusk, Konyek prayed to God for rain, singing with the other boys and girls of the manyatta:

"Fall, rain, fall,
Take the dry skin of the earth
And my thirst;
Fall, rain, fall,
Take the earth's rough hide away,
Bring us milk and grass today."

And the old men of the manyatta, who were as his grandfathers, burnt a special wood called cordia wood, and into the flames they threw a charm given them by a witch-doctor. Then they gathered round the fire and sang the hymn of the old men:

"The black god, ho!" one called out alone.

And the others replied in chorus:

"God, to whom we pray,
Water us this day."

And the one man called out alone again:

"The black god, ho!"

And the others shouted in chorus:

"GO, DROUGHT, GO!
God, God, to whom we pray,
Water, water us this day."

The women sang their hymn, too, and fastened grass to the hems of their skirts. And when still the rain did not fall, Ol-Poruo, who had forseen the drought in his dreams, spoke with the other old men, the Elders, and it was decided that they should visit the witch-doctor. They took two goats as a gift for him, and a calabash of honey-beer; then they departed.

(From *The Calf of the November Cloud* by Hilary Ruben)

About the Passage
1 Where do you think the story is set? Which clues are there in the passage to support this idea?
2 What do you understand the ''red god'' and the ''black god'' to be? Why do you think the author has used these terms?
3 Why do you think the calf of the November Cloud is so special to Konyek?
4 Explain how you think the calf may have got its unusual name.
5 What do you think the ''manyatta'' is? What is a ''calabash''? Try to find out if you are not sure.

Writing
What do you think will happen when the Elders and Ol-Poruo visit the witch-doctor? What will Ol-Poruo say to him? Do you think the witch-doctor will be able to help?
    Write your own ending to the story.

Drought and Flood

Although drought and floods are natural disasters, their effects are often made far more devastating by the acts of man.
    On slopes in some parts of the world huge forests have been cleared to make way for man's ever-increasing population, or to help satisfy his needs for timber. As well as destroying the natural habitat of much of our wildlife, such deforestation invites disaster.
    Trees play a very important part in the balance of life, especially in countries prone to drought and sudden flooding. Their roots go deep into the earth in search of water and in doing so they perform another vital function — they hold the earth in place.
    Without trees to do this the sun bakes the earth, turning it to dust which the wind begins to scatter. When rain eventually falls the remaining topsoil, no longer held in place by tree roots, is washed down the slopes into the valleys, leaving behind huge barren areas. The rivers become choked with this eroded soil and are more likely to flood. This tragic effect is seen all to regularly in countries such as Bangladesh.

Tree roots hold the earth in place

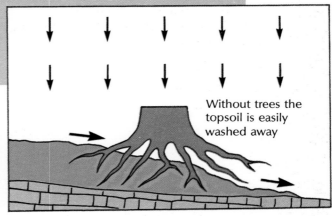
Without trees the topsoil is easily washed away

To think and talk about
1 Explain how the acts of man make the effects of drought and flood more devastating.
2 Can anything be done to prevent this?
3 Discuss the problems which drought and flooding lead to: famine, disease, etc. What can be done to help people who suffer from such disasters?

Finding Out
Deforestation — the removal of forests — is a major concern of ecologists and conservationists. Use your library to find out more about it. Make notes on what you discover.
    Find out about other natural disasters such as earthquakes, hurricanes, volcanic eruptions, etc. How could man reduce the loss of life in such disasters?

Animal Conservation

The Song of the Whale

Heaving mountain in the sea,
Whale, I heard you
Grieving.

Great whale, crying for your life,
Crying for your kind, I knew
How we would use
Your dying:

Lipstick for our painted faces,
Polish for our shoes.
Tumbling mountain in the sea,
Whale, I heard you
Calling.

Bird-high notes, keening, soaring:
At their edge a tiny drum
Like a heartbeat.

We would make you
Dumb.

In the forest of the sea,
Whale, I heard you
Singing,

Singing to your kind.
We'll never let you be.
Instead of life we choose
Lipstick for our painted faces,
Polish for our shoes.

Kit Wright

About the Poem

1 How does the poem make you feel? Give reasons for your answer.
2 What do you think should be done? How would you go about doing it?
3 Find out about the "Save the Whale" movement. How successful has it been?

For Some It's Too Late

Fortunately for the whale, many of its rarer breeds are now officially protected, and although still classed as "endangered" they have a good chance of being saved.

The same cannot be said for the dodo, the quagga or the great auk, all of which are now extinct. Man has hunted and exploited animals and birds for so long that many creatures such as the oryx, the Java rhinoceros and the whooping crane seem doomed to follow the dodo's path.

Activities

1 Choose any two of these vanished or vanishing creatures and find out all you can about them: where they live(d), when, how their numbers were reduced, what they looked like, etc.
2 Write your own poem about an endangered species.

WWF

Planet Earth

Dear Pupils,

I am very pleased to inform you that your group has been selected to be the guest panel of speakers on "Planet Earth", our new series on the environment.

It would be helpful if each member of your group could select one of the following areas as a specialist subject and be prepared to speak for 2-3 minutes on that subject, answering any questions which the audience might ask.

a) Pollution of air and water: its causes, effects and how these effects can be reversed.

b) Pollution of the land: use of pesticides, problems of litter, modern waste and refuse disposal.

c) Animal welfare: how particular animals have become extinct; work of environmental bodies e.g. Greenpeace, World Wide Fund for Nature, etc.

d) Our disappearing world: effects of expansion of mankind: population explosion, deforestation, drought and flood.

As well as stating how these events occur it would be of particular interest if members of the panel could suggest practical ideas and solutions to help with environmental problems.

Thank you for your interest. I look forward to meeting you all next week.

With best wishes,

Yours sincerely, *Alistair McPherson*

Activities

1 Discuss with your group who is going to speak on each of the specialist subjects listed by the producers of *Planet Earth*.
2 Collect and sequence any notes you already have for your specialist subject. Research further where you feel you have insufficient information.
3 Use your notes to write a short 2-3 minute speech. Ask a friend to listen to your speech. Improve your speech if necessary.
4 Appoint someone to act as host for the programme and hold a rehearsal for it. The audience should be ready with their questions. Afterwards make improvements to the speeches, and if necessary carry out more research.
5 Stage the actual programme. You may increase the size of your audience by inviting children from other classes. If you have access to video equipment record the TV programme for later evaluation. If not an audio tape will provide a useful record.
6 Discuss how the programme went. How well did the speakers communicate? Were the audience interested? Do you think everyone gained something from the debate? Are any questions left unanswered? Can answers be found?

The Cry

This painting is called "The Cry". It was painted by Edvard Munch in 1893. Study it carefully and answer these questions.

1 Where do you think the scene is taking place? Which clues in the painting helped you to reach this conclusion?
2 What do you think is happening? Say why you think so.

Writing

Years after finishing this painting Munch wrote a story which seems to refer to his picture.

> "He ran along the sea. The sky and water took on the colour of blood. He heard cries in the air and covered his ears. Earth, sky and sea trembled, and he felt great fear."

Write your own, more detailed, version of Munch's story saying how and why you think the sky and water changed colour, what caused the cries, why the earth trembled and why it was all so terrifying.

Future Worlds

There has been much discussion about what our world will be like in future years. Will we be living in a hygienic, pre-packaged, computerised, automatic world, or will we go back to the simpler life of our forefathers?

Read carefully the passage and poem on these pages. They give us very different glimpses of a future world.

Read this passage carefully, thinking for yourself what the missing word are. Write one word for each space.

You were allowed to walk in the city. Few people did: the moving pavements, the walkways, walked for you. But you could walk if you wished and did not mind the curious stares and the possibility of being stopped by the police and asked to identify and explain yourself.

So Brin walked, barely knowing he was walking. He _____1_____ without seeing the great silver towers, the wide green _____2_____ with each tree named and labelled, each bird and _____3_____ identified on the TV displays. Automatically, he wove his _____4_____ through the pedalecs — the silent electric bicycles that glittered _____5_____ insect-swarms in certain streets and special areas.

Above him, the _____6_____, glassy building soared fifty storeys high, seeming almost to _____7_____ the great transparent curve of the Ecodome that packaged _____8_____ city and made its atmosphere. Around him, the cars _____9_____ and whined, slowly bumbling along the roads, blindly _____10_____ the get-you-there tracks under the road surface. Sometimes a _____11_____ of cars was stopped, each car nudging squishily at the _____12_____ in front; only then did the 'drivers' and passengers _____13_____ up from their in-car TV screens. Sometimes a 'driver' _____14_____ crossly prod the tabs and buttons in front of _____15_____ to make the car go forward again. Of course, _____16_____ made no difference.

Under Brin's feet, the city pumped _____17_____ whirred and hummed and growled and vibrated. Below ground, _____18_____ real business of the city went on — the drains _____19_____ trains, power plants and factories, nature reserves and laboratories, _____20_____ complexes and service depots, protein banks and weathermaker plants . . .

_____21_____ paused, by habit, at one of the city's eight Great _____22_____. This was the second biggest — almost an acre. Trees, _____23_____, waterfowl on the little lake and people, people, people . . .

_____24_____ big coloured moth flew almost into Brin's face, startling _____25_____. Immediately the nearest TV screen showed a still picture _____26_____ the moth and named it, in English and Latin.

'As if I cared,' Brin said.

(From *A Rag, a Bone and a Hank of Hair* by Nicholas Fisk)

To write about

1   Briefly outline the very different views of the future that the poem and the passage describe. Which future would you prefer to happen? Give reasons for your answer.
2   Which view of the future do you think is the most likely? Try to say why you think so.
3   What do you think life will be like in one hundred years' time? Write a detailed description including how these aspects of our lifestyles might have changed. Consider such things as clothing, food, transport, homes and jobs.

Activities

Draw a picture or make a model to illustrate your ideas.

The Horses

Barely a twelvemonth after
The seven days war that put the world to sleep,
Late in the evening the strange horses came.
By then we had made our covenant with silence,
But in the first few days it was so still
We listened to our breathing and were afraid.
On the second day
The radios failed; we turned the knobs; no answer.
On the third day a warship passed us, heading north,
Dead bodies piled on the deck. On the sixth day
A plane plunged over us into the sea. Thereafter
Nothing. The radios dumb;
And still they stand in corners of our kitchens,
And stand, perhaps, turned on, in a million rooms
All over the world. But now if they should speak,
If on a sudden they should speak again,
If on the stroke of noon a voice should speak,
We would not listen, we would not let it bring
That old bad world that swallowed its children quick
At one great gulp. We would not have it again.
Sometimes we think of the nations lying asleep,
Curled blindly in impenetrable sorrow,
And then the thought confounds us with its strangeness.
The tractors lie about our fields; at evening
They look like dank sea-monsters couched and waiting.
We leave them where they are and let them rust:
"They'll moulder away and be like other loam."
We make our oxen drag our rusty ploughs,
Long laid aside. We have gone back
Far past our fathers' land.
                        And then, that evening
Late in the summer the strange horses came.
We heard a distant tapping on the road,
A deepening drumming; it stopped, went on again
And at the corner changed to hollow thunder.
We saw the heads
Like a wild wave charging and were afraid.
We had sold our horses in our fathers' time
To buy new tractors. Now they were strange to us
As fabulous steeds set on an ancient shield
Or illustrations in a book of knights.
We did not dare go near them. Yet they waited,
Stubborn and shy, as if they had been sent
By an old command to find our whereabouts
And that long-lost archaic companionship.
In the first moment we had never a thought
That they were creatures to be owned and used.
Among them were some half-a-dozen colts
Dropped in some wilderness of the broken world,
Yet new as if they had come from their own Eden.
Since then they have pulled our ploughs and borne our loads.
But that free servitude still can pierce our hearts.
Our life is changed; their coming our beginning.
Edwin Muir

Save Our Planet

Design a board game called **Save Our Planet** to teach younger children about the effects of pollution and the need for conservation.

Your game may be a straight-forward counting game, with some risks, like Snakes and Ladders. Alternatively you could make it much more interesting by adding *Hazard Cards* and *Conservation Cards*.

The Hazard Cards would feature pollution hazards and carry penalties, like these:

UNTREATED SEWAGE PUMPED INTO RIVER KILLING WILDLIFE

GO BACK 3 SPACES

HAZARD CARD

POIS...
ES...

M...
3 TURNS

DEFORESTATION IN JUNGLE CAUSES EXTINCTION OF LESSER SPOTTED AARDVARK

GO BACK 5 SPACES

Conservation Cards would carry good news:

CLEAN UP DISUSED CANAL

TAKE AN EV...

ESTABLISH A SANCTUARY FOR RARE BREEDS OF WATER FOWL

...VE ON 3 SPACES

CONSERVATION CARD

Make your board as interesting and as colourful as possible. It doesn't have to be rectangular. You could make your board in the shape of an endangered species, a litter bin, a factory chimney or even the shape of the earth!

Think of suitable shapes for your counters. Don't forget to include a set of simple instructions which younger players will find easy to follow.